UNTIMELY DEATHS
BY ASSASSINATION

UNTIMELY DEATHS
BY ASSASSINATION

BY

WALTER J. WHITTEMORE JR.

iUniverse, Inc.
Bloomington

UNTIMELY DEATHS BY ASSASSINATION

iUniverse books may be ordered through booksellers or by contacting:

iUniverse
1663 Liberty Drive
Bloomington, IN 47403
www.iuniverse.com
1-800-Authors (1-800-288-4677)

ISBN: 978-1-4620-3822-0 (sc)
ISBN: 978-1-4620-3824-4 (hc)
ISBN: 978-1-4620-3823-7 (ebk)

Printed in the United States of America

iUniverse rev. date: 02/02/2012

DEDICATION

THIS BOOK IS DEDICATED TO my five children, Carol, Jim, Steve, Barbara and Bette, and also my deceased wife Constance (Connie) and my present wife, Yvonne, who had been very patient and understanding, realizing that I was engrossed in doing research and writing for hours which took away time usually devoted to her and her interests.

ACKNOWLEDGEMENT

THIS AUTHOR CAN'T SAY ENOUGH about his daughter, Barbara Tueichi, who did all the typing and spent hours doing the retyping of the errors that were made in the original draft.

INTRODUCTION

ONE MAY ASK WHY WOULD a person write about people who were assassinated. The answer is simple—intrigue and fascination. After writing and doing research for my previous book titled, <u>World Battles and Their Leaders Who Changed Global History</u>, I stumbled across important and diabolic characters who left their mark on society. This was the stimulus which provoked my idea for writing this book which involved hours of research. However, the result was most gratifying as I learned a great deal of the lives of celebrities, good and bad, which caused an upheaval of emotions, sadness, bitterness, and retaliation.

These men and women were usually intelligent human beings who had high moral standards and who made contributions to society. Others were immoral, cruel, belligerent, and hostile who did more damage than anyone would ever imagine from a person relegated to a high office of administration.

People, such as, Mahatma Gandhi, Martin Luther King, fall into that category of fine, moral standards; whereas, such people, as Caligula and Caracalla, Roman emperors, were immoral, cruel, and dissident. Caligula, for instance, announced his divinity and demanded divine worship; his counterpart, Caracalla murdered his brother, Geta.

The assassinations of these individuals brings to my mind two outstanding people who were spared from this diabolic act and survived gun shot wounds, namely, President Ronald Reagan and John Paul II, pope of the Roman Catholic Church.

As a final word, my intention was to give an account, even though briefly at times, of these outstanding individuals whose lives were snuffed out before their time. Who knows what great accomplishments they would have achieved if they were spared a few more years. Also, where available the names of these assassins and their motives for killing were addressed.

It is my hope and desire that the reader will enjoy the lives of these magnificent people who left their mark on society and in history.

To make for easy reading, I have arranged these persons in a chronological manner according to the dates of their assassination.

As a final word, although there are a whole host of people, notable and notorious, which are not included in this book, nevertheless, this author felt that those written about were interesting, informative, and intriguing which the reader, I'm sure, will enjoy.

CONTENTS

XERXES I—465 B.C.

XERXES WAS BORN ABOUT 520 B.C. and was the eldest son of Darius I and Queen Atossa. Darius I was the grandson of Cyrus the Great the great ruler of the Persian Empire which was one of the most important empires in the southwest of Asia at that time.

In 486 he faced rebellions in Babylonia and Egypt which he ruthlessly suppressed before he invaded Greece.

The Persians had built a bridge of boats across the Hellespont, the present day Dardanelles, and dug a canal across the Mount Athos peninsula to avoid a repetition of the disaster to the fleet of Darius in 492 before their invasion of Greece.

After the Persian defeat at the Battle of Marathon in 490 B.C. and his naval defeat at the Battle of Salamis, Xerxes sought revenge and regrouped his army during the winter months and returned to Greece in the spring of 479 B.C. and was thoroughly defeated by the Greek hoplite soldiers at Plataea. This outstanding defeat at Plataea was the beginning of the final collapse of the Persian Empire.

Alexander the Great, the son of Philip II of Macedonia, defeated the Persian emperor, Darius III, in the Battle of Issus in 333 B.C. and this was the coup de grace of the Persian Empire.

In 465 B.C., Xerxes was assassinated in a palace intrigue and his son, Artaxerxes took over the reins of government.

It has been said that the Battle of Plataea was one of the most important events in world history, in that, if Xerxes prevailed in that battle, Greece would have been dominated under Persian rule, and Persian, rather than Greek literature, influence, and art, would have prevailed over Western philosophy and education.

PHILIP II, KING OF MACEDONIA—336 B.C.

WHEN READING ABOUT THE KINGS of Macedonia, it is most extraordinary to learn that all three kings were assassinated—Alexander, Perdikkas, and Philip who were all brothers.

Of all three, Philip II emerged as the greatest warrior king who became fascinated with Greek culture and tried to put his country on a same par with it.

At the age of fifteen, Philip was taken to Thebes by his captors as a hostage because they feared his brother; King Alexander had leanings toward the takeover of Thebes.

While Philip was there, he was highly impressed with Greek knowledge and their culture. Therefore, he engaged himself with their philosophy, literature, and military tactics.

While he was stationed there, his brother, King Alexander was assassinated and he was succeeded to the throne by Perdikkas who was also assassinated. These incidents turned out to be a struggle as to whom would succeed in becoming the next ruler of Macedonia.

At age forty-six, Philip had seven wives. His favorite wife was Olympias who was the mother of that famous general, Alexander the Great.

However, Eurydice, his seventh wife, had supplanted Olympias as his favorite. Eurydice later gave birth to a son which Olympias felt would jeopardize her son's chances of becoming the next king.

Worried about her life, Olympias decided to flee from the court.

Philip, being a staunch warrior, had plans to invade Asia and attack his rival, Persia. To do this, he needed extra men for the task. He, then, set out to conquer Thebes and several other Greek cities but, he left Athens untouched. The reason given—he wished to incorporate Athens large fleet which he needed for the invasion.

While he planned the invasion of Persia, he took a trip to Aegae, the ancient capital of Macedonia. Rumors had it that Philip was planning another marriage and possibly another heir. This talk naturally alienated his wife Olympias still further, and also, his son, Alexander. To prevent further rumors, he reconciled his differences with Alexander and assured him that he did not intend to jeopardize his succession to the throne.

At the wedding of Philip's daughter, the tragedy took place. Philip, displaying his bravery and lack of fear of his people, proceeded in front of his bodyguards.

It was at this point in time that a noble named Pausanias leaped forward and plunged a dagger beneath his ribs.

As the assassin tried to escape, he tripped over a vine and was wrestled to the ground. He was then shackled with clamps to his arms, legs, and neck, and dragged to the arena. Here, he was left to starve to death.

There have been several accounts given for the assassination.

One such reason was that Pausanias had a caustic grievance against the queen's uncle, Attalus, and also against Philip because he failed to provide justice.

Another reason written by Aristotle, the Greek tutor of Alexander, implied that Pausanias had a homosexual relationship with Philip and that they were lovers.

Aristotle, in his book, <u>Politics</u>, defended Alexander and his mother for their involvement in the killing of Philip by stating that the king was killed for personal reasons rather than for his rule of the kingdom.

However, this view of Aristotle has been taken lightly by contemporaries because of his close association with Alexander while he was tutoring him.

Last, but not least, was the involvement of Olympias and her son Alexander in the plot to get rid of Philip in order to place Alexander on the throne while Eurydice's son was still an infant.

Philip II has gone down in history as a great, proud, warrior king who had great ambitions as exemplified by his conquest of Greek cities, the making of his capital, Pella, a great cultural center, his improvement of the strength of the nation's military, and his uniting of the Greek people. He was also a patron of the arts. In 1977, a collection of golden objects were found in his grave to verify this.

However, his one big dream was to conquer Persia but, he was assassinated before he was able to accomplish this great feat.

Nevertheless, his son, Alexander took up the task and achieved this dream by subduing the Persians when he crossed the Hellespont into Asia.

DARIUS III OF PERSIA—330 B.C.

DARIUS III WAS THE LAST king of the Achaemenid Empire of Persia. Codomannus was his real name but, later, took the regna name Darius III. Darius was a distant relative of the royal house who made a name for himself in a war against the Cadusii. At the time of this battle, he was courier serving the royal family.

Darius' father was Arsames and his mother Sisygambis. He believed in the religion of Zoroastrianism.

How he came to power is most extraordinary. A vizier, named Bagoas who was a eunuch, had previously poisoned Darius' two predecessors, Artaxerxes III and his son Arses, and when he realized that Darius would not cave in to his whims, he decided to poison him also. However, Darius discovered from several informants about the plot to end his life, and forced Bagoas to drink the poison.

Darius' reign was riddled with all sorts of problems, mostly with his provinces. The unreliable satraps were rebellious and caused a great deal of hardships. One such troublemaker was the satrap of Egypt, Khabash. Egypt had proclaimed its independence following the death of Artaxerxes III. However, the real problem was with Philip II of Macedonia. He was authorized by the League of Corinth to take action against Persia because they burned and looted the Athenian temples during the Second Persian War.

The Persians had been invading the Ionian cities along the coast of Asia Minor for quite some time, and eventually, took command of them.

In order to oust them, Philip II sent a force of hoplites into Asia Minor under two outstanding generals, Attalus and Parmenion. Philip was, unexpectedly, assassinated during this campaign when he was celebrating his daughter's wedding in Macedonia. While entering a theater, Pausanias, a guard, stabbed him under his ribs.

Philip's son, Alexander (called the Great because of his outstanding victories), became the ruler of Macedonia and the Greek city-states and, invaded Asia Minor. He immediately defeated the Persians at the Battle of the Granicus. During the foray, Darius III decided to stay at home in Persepolis and let his satraps do battle having confidence in their ability to stop the onslaught.

Later, in the Battle of Issus in 333 B.C., in which Darius took part, despite the enormity of his forces, he lost the battle and was forced to flee in his chariot.

Alexander captured Darius' headquarters and also captured his family.

Darius wrote letters to Alexander pleading with him to release his family. However, he was unable to convince the adamant Alexander to release them.

Alexander's bargain consisted of Darius' acknowledgment of Alexander as the Emperor of Persia, and if so, he would release them.

It was during this period of warfare that Darius' wife, Statira, died during childbirth.

The last battle, which he engaged in, was at Gaugamela in 331 B.C. where he had assembled a large army including the armies of several of his satraps. Despite its size, the army took a huge beating and Darius, just as he did at Issus, was forced to flee in a chariot leaving behind his property and soldiers to be taken by Alexander.

It has been estimated that the Persians lost between 40,000 and 90,000 men in the battle.

Darius then fled to Ecbatana where he tried to raise a third army. In the meantime, Alexander captured Susa, Babylon, and Persepolis, the Persian capital.

Darius was unable to raise an army in eastern Iran because his authority had diminished; also, Alexander's liberal policy of submission was very tempting in contrast to the alternative of Persian domination.

Because of all this adverse publicity, his popularity took a tumble and he soon realized that his empire was quickly being swept away.

It was after the great battle at Gaugamela that a loyal friend, Bessus, the satrap of Bactria (modern Afghanistan), betrayed him. At nighttime, the Bactrians surrounded a tent which housed the emperor, chained him and carried him off to Bactria.

As Alexander closed in after his pursuit of Darius, Bessus stabbed Darius to death and left his body in a wagon which was later found by one of the Macedonian soldiers.

Alexander, as a kind gesture, sent Darius' body back to Persepolis for burial.

Alexander, later married Darius' daughter Statira II at Opis in 324 B.C.

Bessus, who had killed Darius III, took the name Artaxerxes V and called himself the King of Persia. Alexander captured him and, after he was tortured, had him executed.

Darius has gone done in history as being a coward and an incapable despot who was selfish and didn't care for the welfare of his citizens. His cowardness was shown several times when he fled from the scene of battle at Issus and Gaugemela in a chariot leaving behind his soldiers and his property.

GAIUS JULIUS CAESAR—44B.C.

CAESAR WAS THE SON OF a patrician family who extended the frontiers of the Roman Empire further than any other Roman emperor had ever done before. Caesar has been regarded as a quintessential Roman emperor, even though Rome was still a republic when he was young and that office of emperor wasn't created until after his death. Having entered the Roman army, he served in Asia and earned the Civic Crown which was the highest medal of valor at that time. He entered politics after his stint in Asia and took the office of state treasurer. Later, he became chief preistat and moved up in status to a consulship when he was only forty-three years of age.

In the history of warfare, not many militants come close to his achievements.

In 58 B.C., he entered Cisalpine Gaul as a proconsul to defend Rome's borders in the north. This protection was necessary as Gaul's soldiers had sacked Rome in 390 B.C.

Caesar, however, had other grandiose ideas. He contemplated an expansion of the Roman Empire's borders through Gaul and on to the North Sea.

Between 58 and 55 B.C., Caesar conquered Gaul (France), Belgica (Belgium), and Helvetii (Switzerland). Later, he fought the Germanic tribes across the Rhine River. He, also, crossed the English Channel and invaded Britain claiming most of its territory.

In conquering Gaul, Caesar had two factors in his favor: Gallic division, as the Gauls were divided into a whole host of quarreling tribes; Germanic aggression, as they were constantly invading Gaul and taking supplies and territory.

Therefore, Caesar used the excuse that he had to stop the invasion of the Helvetti, (a German tribe) into Gaul. Caesar was successful in that he prevented any more incursions into Gallic territory. He, also, added some Gallic territory to Rome's domain.

In 57 B.C., Caesar was engaged in another battle. This time, the enemy was the belligerent Nervii tribe located in present day Belgium.

As stated previously, being not satisfied with these conquests, he decided to cross the English Channel and invade Britain.

The Gauls because of Caesar's invasions finally united under a new and capable leader, Vercingetorix, chief of the Arverni tribe.

The Gauls were then able to finally stop the incursion of Caesar troops at the stronghold of the city of Gergovia. After losing a battle on an open plain, the tribe retreated to Alexia where they were surrounded by an estimated 50,000 Roman soldiers.

Realizing that the situation was hopeless, Vercingetorix surrendered in 52 B.C. which finally brought the Gallic Wars to a close.

After all these escapades, Caesar returned to Rome a national hero but ran into a political conflict with his advisory, Pompey, the Roman general who had taken Jerusalem.

At this time, Pompey held the position of Chief Consul. Caesar, envious of Pompey's position, demanded that he should be given the consulship. Instead, it had been given to Pompey which caused a great deal of enmity between the two.

In 50 B.C., Caesar flaunted the law that required generals not to bring their armies into Rome but they were required to keep them north of the Rubicon River.

He brazenly crossed the Rubicon and entered Rome and formed a coup to depose Pompey. He, also, dissolved the republic and made himself dictator.

After this arrangement, he marched into Greece and made it a part of the Roman Empire. Not happy or content with this victory, he entered in Egypt and Syria and captured these two countries.

In 46 B.C., he returned to Rome and became dictator for life.

On March 15, 44 B.C., the Senate recognizing Caesar's position as being too powerful, had Caesar's loyal friends, Cassius and Brutus, assassinate him in the Senate.

Caesar is noted for overthrowing the republic and creating the office of emperor. His nephew, Caesar Augustus, made the republic official after his uncle's death fourteen years later.

Caesar has gone down in history, not only as a great emperor, but also, as a great general, who expanded Rome's empire in Europe and the Middle East.

He is also known as a great writer, because he gives us a clear picture of his military campaigns in seven books called <u>De Bello Gallico,</u> (The Gallic Wars). His histories of these and the civil wars have also been called <u>Commentaries</u>.

MARCUS TULLIUS CICERO—43 B.C.

CICERO WAS BORN IN 106 B.C. in Arpinum, south of Rome. Cicero's father was a wealthy equestrian who had good relations with the elite in Rome. Because of his disability (a semi-invalid), he didn't participate in public life. However, he compensated for his disability by engaging in various studies.

Cicero's mother was Helvia and not much is known about her private life except her interest and control of their house which was the responsibility of Roman wives at that time. She was regarded as a thrifty housewife according to her son, Quintus.

The speaking of Latin and Greek in Rome during this period was considered culturally favorable by the upper classes. Cicero fell into this category, as he was educated in the teachings of the ancient Greek poets, historians and philosophers. The Greeks in ancient time excelled in oratory. Cicero, being knowledgeable in the Greek language, was thus able to translate the works of Greek philosophers which garnered large audiences and ignited his reputation.

According to Plutarch, the Greek biographer, Cicero's education and learning proved fruitful as he gained the opportunity to study Roman law under Quintus Mucius Scaevola.

While studying law, Cicero gained many friends. One, in particular, was a famous lawyer, Servius Sulpicius Rufus, and another, Titus Pomponius. The latter became Cicero's adviser and longtime friend. Later, Pomponius was given the cognomen "Atticus."

Cicero, in 83-81 B.C., commenced his career as a lawyer. In 80 B.C. he defended Sextus Roscius who was charged of parricide (the killing of one's father or parents). This was his first important case.

The result was the acquittal of Roscius. Cicero, endangered himself by accusing Chrysogonus, a friend of Sulla, of the crime. Sulla, a Roman general, could have easily murdered Cicero for prosecuting Chrysogonus for the crime.

Fearing Sulla's enmity, Cicero traveled to Greece. In Athens, he met his longtime friend, Atticus, who introduced him to some very important people. While there, he was introduced to the rhetorician, Apollonius Molon of Rhodes. He refined Cicero's style of oratory which changed his performance in speaking and his outlook in rhetoric.

Inspired by the Athenian philosophy of Plato and other great Greek philosophers, Cicero introduced their philosophy to the Roman citizenry, thereby, creating in Latin a vocabulary of philosophical Greek words. Nevertheless, even though Cicero worshipped Plato for his political and moral endeavors, he rejected his theory of Ideas.

Then, in 79 B.C., Cicero married Terentia. The marriage lasted some 30 years and was regarded as a happy one. She came from a wealthy family of noble birth which delighted Cicero as it vaulted his political ambitions both socially and economically. She was a common person socially and very pious. She was also a very adamant wife who took a strong interest in the affairs of her husband's political career. However, the marriage finally faltered and Cicero and Terentia departed—the divorce took place in 45 B.C.

In 46 B.C. Cicero met and married Publilia, a very young girl who had been his ward. This marriage, however, didn't last long. It has been recorded that Cicero married her for her money because he had to pay for Terentia's dowry.

Cicero had a daughter named Tullia and he showed her a huge amount of affection. A tragedy took place in February of 45 B.C. when Tullia became ill and died after giving birth to a son in January. Cicero's grief was tremendous.

Atticus, his close friend, told him to come for a visit in order to squelch his bereavement. While there, Cicero took advantage of Atticus's library and read the great works of Greek philosophers about overcoming grief. However, this reading didn't console him in his sorrow.

Cicero's son, Marcus wanted a military career in contrast to Cicero's desire that he become a philosopher.

Marcus, in defiance, joined Pompey's army in 49 B.C. Caesar pardoned him for his involvement in Pompey's army after Pompey was defeated in 48 B.C. at Pharsalus.

Instead of going to Athens where his father sent him to study under the peripatetic philosopher, Kratippos in 48 B.C., he went on a binge and had a good time. After Cicero was murdered, he joined the <u>Liberatores</u> and was later forgiven by Augustus for his participation.

Augustus elevated Marcus' career and had him appointed augur and later consul in 30 B.C. He was later given the proconsulship of the province of Asia and Syria.

Cicero was a prolific writer. Many of his works have survived—<u>On The Republic</u> and <u>On The Laws</u>. Of his speeches, only fifty-eight survived out of eighty-eight which were recorded.

Politically, Cicero won fame and held various positions in administration. In 75 B.C., he was the quaestor in western Sicily. He gained a reputation there and was asked by the Sicilians to prosecute the governor of Sicily, Gaius Verres who was corrupt and who plundered the Sicilians.

Because of his success in this case, Cicero gained a reputation in Rome as being the greatest orator that Rome ever had.

Cicero grew up at a time when civil wars were prevalent. Sulla, a great Roman general and dictator, won a victory in the first of many civil wars. His reforms, however, gave more power to the equestrian class which increased their political power and station.

Cicero was a Roman constitutionalist as well as a novus homo and an Italian eques. He was instrumental in ascending the Roman cursus honorum where each magistrate was held at or near the youngest age. He, also, served as president of the Reclamation (extortion) Court. At age of 43, he was elected consul. By these various appointments, his career as a politician took an upward swing which improved his status in the hierarchy of nobility.

In 63 B.C., he was elected Consul. While in this position, he neutralized a conspiracy to overthrow the Roman Republic led by Lucias Sergius Catiline. His four acidulous speeches, called the "Catiline Orations," were the spark which ignited the emotions of the populace which drove the culprit from the city.

Catiline fled the city and relied on his followers to start the revolution within the city. Catiline tried to ally himself with a tribe from Transalpine Gaul, called the Allobroges to participate in the plot but, Cicero while associating with the Gaul's was able to seize letters which involved the conspirators. In the midst of the Senate floor, they were forced to confess their crimes. The Senate wanted to invoke the extreme penalty but, Julius

Caesar convinced them that it would set a precedent and he favored life imprisonment instead. Because of Cato's speech (a Roman statesman) in which he favored the death penalty, the Senate finally consented to it. The conspirators were taken to the Roman prison, Tullianum, where they were strangled. Cicero received the <u>Pater Patrial</u> for his magnificent job in suppressing the conspiracy. Thereafter, he lived in fear because he had put a Roman citizen to death without the convenience of a fair trial.

Then, in 60 B.C., Julius Caesar asked Cicero if he would become the fourth member with his cohorts, Pompey and Marcus Licinius Crassus. This group eventually became the First Triumvirate. However, because he thought that this union would undermine the Republic, he refused the invitation.

Then, in 58 B.C., Cicero ran into trouble because of his involvement in the death of the conspirators who were condemned without a trial. Publius Clodius Pulcher, the tribune of the plebs, had a law enacted which would exile anyone who executed a Roman citizen without a trial. Not receiving any assurance from Pompey or the Senate which would mitigate him from any punishment, he went into exile and headed for Thessalonica, Greece, on May 23rd, 58 B.C. While there, he became depressed and contemplated suicide. Atticus, however, stepped in and convinced him that this wasn't the way to solve his problems. Then, he got a break when Titus Annius Milo became the newly elected tribune. His defense of Cicero resulted in the Senate voting unanimously in favor of recalling Cicero from exile. Cicero was able to return to Italy on August 5th, 57 B.C.

His daughter, Tullia, was there to greet him besides a roaring crowd.

In 56 B.C., Cicero forfeited his entrance into politics and spent most of his time reading literary books.

During the civil war in Rome in 50 B.C., Caesar took Rome without a fight. Pompey, his rival, fled the city with Caesar in hot pursuit. It was at this time that Cicero favored Pompey and traveled with him to Pharsalus in 48 B.C.

Pompey was defeated by Caesar at Pharsalus and Cicero returned to Rome. Caesar, being merciful, pardoned Cicero for his attachment with Pompey.

After Caesar's murder on the Ides of March, Cicero and Mark Antony became the two leading men in Rome but they were unfriendly toward each other. When Octavian, Caesar's heir and adopted son, became emperor of Rome, Cicero gave a series of speeches in which he attacked Antony for his false interpretations of Caesar's intentions. These speeches have been called the <u>Philippics</u> which refer to the denunciation of Philip II of Macedon by the Greek, Demosthenes.

Cicero urged the Senate to call Antony a state enemy. This exclamation was later fulfilled when he was declared an enemy of the state when he refused to lift the siege of Mutina which was occupied by Decimus Brutus. However, Cicero failed in his plan to drive out Antony.

After Octavian formed the Second Triumvirate consisting of Antony, Lepidus and himself, they began to list their enemies and rivals. Cicero and his supporters were among those listed as enemies of the state. However, Octavian argued that Cicero shouldn't have been on the list. Despite his argument for Cicero's release from the list, Cicero was hunted down. Cicero was caught on December 7th, 43 B.C. while leaving his home in Formiae in a litter going to the coast where he was to embark on a ship to Macedonia. When the assassins, Herennius a centurion, and Popillius a tribune, arrived, Philologus, a free slave of Cicero's brother Quintus Cicero, betrayed Cicero's whereabouts by supplying the necessary information.

According to Plutarch's account, Herennius first slew him, and then cut off his head. Antony had his hands cut off. According to tradition whereby Sulla and Marius had the heads of their enemies displayed in the Forum, Antony had Cicero's head and hands nailed and put on display on the Rostra in the Roman Forum.

According to Cassius Dio, a Roman historian, a story is told in which Antony's wife, Fulvia, took Cicero's head, pulled out his tongue, and jabbed it repeatedly with her hairpin.

Such was the case in Roman times, when brutality was in the forefront on many occasions.

It can be truthfully elaborated, despite his vacillations in political matters and alliances, Cicero stuck to his belief in constitutional law despite the pressures of autocratic senatorial beliefs and emperor's forceful tactics.

Cicero has gone down in history as a great writer, philosopher, lawyer, orator and an outstanding statesman. Also, he distinguished himself as a competent translator and linguist.

GAIUS CAESAR GERMANICUS (CALIGULA)—41 A.D.

CALIGULA HAS GONE DOWN IN history as one of the most eccentric, cruel, incestuous emperors that ever took the Roman crown. His escapades with prostitutes and homosexuals were abominable. If he didn't like someone or whoever disagreed with him, he eliminated them quickly. He was a spendthrift as evidence has shown him spending all the sesterces in the treasury—money which had accumulated when Tiberius was emperor due to his skillful management of money. In order to keep up his extravagant activities, he taxed the wages of his citizens; had a sales tax on food; and taxed the earnings of prostitutes.

His actions, at times, were intolerable. He accused the rich of treason and had them executed so that the treasury could collect their fortunes.

His extravagance knew no bounds. Stories have it that he bathed in perfume instead of water. The banquets which he gave cost millions of sesterces.

He went so far as to say he was a deity.

Caligula had sex relations with all three of his sisters. He forced his sister Drusilla to divorce her husband so that he could marry her. If he fancied any beautiful married woman, he would send letters of divorce to her in her husband's name so that he could have an affair with her.

Regardless of his marriage, (he was married four times), he found the time to have homosexual relations with other men.

Caligula had been brought up in army camps and he was given this name at an early age, derived from "caligal" military boots, the little boots which he wore. His predecessor was the excellent general, Tiberius, who was his uncle and who retired to the isle of Capri where he imbibed heavily and eventually became mad.

Caligula abolished treason trials and became a generous person during the early stages of his reign. At this time, he became very popular with the populace.

However, this jovial and benevolent emperor became hopelessly mad while spending only six months of his reign.

This madness, some say, was due to a serious illness. During this period of his reign, he became cruel and capricious. Many died for any and no reason at all—his whims went amok on many occasions.

His fears when he was sick became insurmountable. For instances, when it thundered, he would hide under his bed and, other times, he prowled through his house at night crying for day-light. Sometimes he joked, such as, the time when he said that he would make his horse, Incitatus consul during a dinner engagement.

Caligula disregarded human life on many occasions. Once, while he was sparring with a gladiator using a wooden sword, the gladiator deliberately went down. Caligulas, in a fit of rage, pulled a dagger and stabbed him to death. His heartlessness was displayed at another time when he was told that the price of raw meat for the animals had risen; he nonchalantly stated the criminals would do just as well.

It is ironic that he had received the throne due to the efforts of a prefect of the Praetorian Guard named Macro, who had assassinated the emperor, Tiberius, by smothering him. He became a trusted and capable adviser of Caligula. Caligula had Macro killed for a reason which no one knows.

Caligula had at one time become very popular with the Praetorian Guards but, after witnessing his capricious cruelties and excesses, he lost their confidence and trustworthiness.

The end finally came and his life was cut short by a tribune of the Praetorian Guard, Cassius Chaerea who had to see the emperor each morning to be told the password for the day. Caligula ridiculed him and made fun of him because he had a high-pitched voice. Caligula referred to him as "girl". Because of Caligula's humiliating behavior, Chaerea plotted the emperor's murder.

Then, one day, Chaerea and several guards assassinated Caligula in a secret passage in the palace. They stabbed him several times with their swords until he fell to the floor.

The Guards then proceeded to the imperial palace where they found Caligula's wife, Caesonia with her small daughter, Drusilla. The mother was struck with a sword and fell to the floor in a bloody heap. Then, one of the guards lifted the young child and flung her against a wall which crushed her skull.

Another emperor's life was cut short before his time. Caligula had served only four years.

Suetonius, a Roman historian, described him very eloquently when he stated that Caligula was a "cruel, arrogant and extravagant ruler" whose reign lasted only four years and was administered in an inconsistent and incongruous manner.

CLAUDIUS—54 A.D.

CLAUDIUS WAS BORN ON AUGUST 1ˢᵗ, 10 B.C. at Lugdunum in Gaul. He was the third emperor of the Julio-Claudian dynasty. He was the son of Drusus Claudius Nero and Antonia, the daughter of Mark Antony. His uncle, Tiberius, became emperor in 14 A.D. Unfortunately, Claudius was born with physical defects. He was constantly debilitated—stuttered, limped and drooled. These defects were an embarrassment to his family and they kept him isolated from the public during his childhood and youth. During his period of adolescence, he occupied himself by reading works of liberal arts, concentrating mostly on history.

By studying history, he developed the necessary knowledge and skills which were needed in the administration of government.

Claudius witnessed family tragedies at an early age—father died when campaigning, and his brother, Germanicus, died A.D. 19, under unknown but secret circumstances. His sister, Livilla, died when she had a relationship with Sejanus who was also "eliminated" in 31 A.D. Despite these tragedies, Claudius survived.

At the age of 46 years, Claudius received a position as a consul by his cruel and heartless nephew, Caligula. This act was a sheer joke on the part of Caligula who took delight in inflicting harsh jokes on his uncle. This position was Claudius first public office.

How Claudius procured the throne and became emperor of Rome has involved several dubious stories, mostly speculation. The one which this author seems more substantial is the one in which some Praetorian Guardsmen found Claudius hiding behind a curtain after the assassination of his nephew, Caligula.

At first, the Senate was hesitant in honoring Claudius as the emperor and were even contemplating building an army to confront the Guard militarily. However, after their troops deserted to the Praetorian Guard, they realized the hopelessness of the situation and proceeded to the Camp to show their respect to Claudius's appointment.

It is interesting to note that this intrusion of the military in politics was the first outstanding move in that direction.

The election of the emperor set a precedent which became rather routine in that the military took an active part in the selection of emperors and not the consensus of government officials.

This procedure entailed military loyalty and if this didn't occur, the power of the emperor was diminished and sometimes accompanied by the loss of his life.

Thus, Claudius's reign set a course of security and peace. His first act of administration was to apprehend and execute the assassins of Caligula.

To show that he was interested in the centrality of the military to his position, he embarked on an expedition into Britain in the summer 43 A.D. This was followed by a victory parade at Colchester and he, later, departed for Rome to celebrate this triumph in 44 A.D.

Claudius' reputation and stance were looked upon by the aristocracy in a frivolous and ingenious way because of his selection and association with the military. This political arrangement placed him on an inferior status with the elite senatorial aristocracy who regarded him as a usurper. Claudius trusted ex-slaves more than he did the callous and self-centered aristocracy.

Therefore, his reign is regarded as the first era of the exalted imperial freedmen.

Claudius, in 38 A.D., married Valeria Messalina who came from a noble family. They had two children, a daughter named Octavia and a son, Britannicus. She was identified as a nymphomaniac who on various occasions held wild parties. She even had her former lovers put to death or those who rejected her amorous advances.

These wild parties, her sexual advances in the political sphere, and her advances on courtiers, diminished her reputation. Because of one of these wild parties held at the palace in which a marriage ceremony was performed between Silius, a consul-designate, and herself, she, Silius and others of the performance were summarily executed.

This in turn, provoked a mad scramble among the freedmen who tried to get Claudius to select one of their candidates as his new bride. Due to Pallas's influence, Claudius married Agrippina the Younger.

She was the daughter of Claudius's brother, Germanicus. She had been married before and had a son, Nero, whom she wished to be the future emperor of Rome.

Claudius took a liking to Nero and adopted him as his son on February 25th, 50 A.D. He took Nero to circus games and showed him a great deal of affection. Who would have known that this crazed person would eventually kill his mother and wife and set fire to Rome.

In administering Romes' provinces, he showed his capability by rendering a direct approach over "client kingship." However, when it came to judicial matters, he was unmercifully criticized for his flamboyant interference with judicial cases—not paying attention to both sides of a case, making outrageous rulings on others, and hearing special cases behind closed-doors with only his personal advisors in attendance.

By these obnoxious actions, he, definitely, made a mockery of the judicial system in Rome.

In his building activities, he made great strides. He had a new aqueduct built for the city of Rome, drainage of the Fucine Lake, and also, a new port at Portus.

Suetonius, a great historian, ably summarizes his construction of public works when he stated: "his public works were grandiose and necessary rather than numerous."

From the outset, Claudius' wives were a burden to him, especially, his fourth wife, Agrippina who got rid of him by putting poison in his mushrooms. After an agony of twelve ungodly hours, he died.

Claudius was regarded as an enigmatic individual but his attributes and successes were many. He was an intelligent human being and had a keen respect for tradition. He was looked upon as being timid, careful and aware of what was going on about him. However, at times, he was cruel and unsympathetic, killing those who opposed him and taking delight in the slaughter of men in the gladiatorial games. His successes rested in the management of client kingdoms, good management of government in the Roman provinces, and last, but not least, the invasion of Britain in which he took part.

Thus, came to an abrupt climax the life of an emperor who believed his major objective was the ascendancy of the Roman Empire.

AGRIPPINA THE YOUNGER—59 A.D.

AFTER READING THE LIFE OF Agrippina the Younger, there aren't enough adjectives to describe this woman's character. She was vicious, ambitious, calculating, merciless, ruthless, heartless and violent. She had a passion for power and used any means or methods to obtain it. She also, used her three marriages to enhance her chance of securing it.

Her first marriage entailed an arrangement by the emperor Tiberius to wed Gnaeus Domitius Ahenobarbus who came from a wealthy and distinguished family. This marriage was to take place in Rome.

The second marriage was with Gaius Sallustius Crispus Passienus who was an influential, powerful and wealthy man and who was consul several times. However, little has been known of their relationship.

The third marriage, which took place on New Year's Day in 49 A.D., was with Emperor Claudius who was crowned emperor by the Praetorian Guards after they had assassinated the tyrant, Caligula.

Some of Claudius' actions were brutal and unsavory. The historian Suetonius said his disposition was one of "cruelty and sanguinary". His executions were many—Cneius Pompey, his eldest daughter's husband, 300 knights, 35 senators, and Appius Silanus, father of his son-in-law.

Because of these crimes of humanity, he became very unpopular with the Roman citizens.

Agrippina's marriage was not for love but for the attainment of power. This was displayed most prominently when her son Lucius (Nero) became emperor and she had the reins of government in her hands.

She was the first daughter of her mother, Agrippina the Elder and her father, Germanicus who was a famous general and politician. Germanicus was a favorite of his great-uncle, Augustus. He wanted Germanicus to succeed his uncle Tiberius who was Augustus's own adopted son and heir.

In the year 19 A.D., Germanicus died and rumors of murder pervaded the Roman populace pointing to his wife, Agrippina the Elder as the instigator because she had returned to Rome with his ashes.

Agrippina the Younger, after the death of her father was taken into the custody of her mother and great-grandmother, Livia. She was housed on the Palatine Hill in Rome. She was surrounded by influential and notable people here, especially, when Tiberius became emperor and the head of the family after Augustus died.

As it was mentioned previously, Tiberius, her great uncle, had arranged her first marriage to Domitius which was celebrated in Rome. He was wealthy but his character was disreputable and base.

Caligula became emperor when Tiberius died in March, 37 A.D. It was during this time that Julia Agrippina, his sister, gained influence and notoriety.

Agrippina had a son and she and Domitius decided to name him Lucius Domitius Ahenobarbus after Domitius's late father. In time, he grew up to be the future emperor of Rome and he was called Nero.

Emperor Caligula was a perverted individual who had incestuous acts with his sisters. He, also, permitted his friends to sleep with his sisters, Julia Drusilla and Julia Livilla in the palace.

Then, in 39 A.D., Agrippina, Livilla, and Marcus Lepidus, Drusilla's widower, decided to murder Caligula. However, this plot failed. The motive was to have Lepidus become the new emperor.

Caligula showed evidence of the plot by producing handwritten letters which illustrated the method they were going to use to kill him. Caligula had Lepidus executed and Livilla and her sister Agrippina were exiled to the Pontine Islands.

Caligula, his wife Caesonia, and his daughter were murdered on January 24th, 41 A.D. Claudius, Agrippina's uncle, became the new emperor or Rome.

One of his first moves was to order the return of Agrippina and her sister Livilla from exile.

Caludius, because of his benevolence, had Lucius's (Nero's) inheritance reinstated. He, also, was instrumental in getting a divorce for Gaius Sallustius Cripus so that he could marry Agrippina. Cripsus was a powerful, wealthy man who had served twice as consul. He was very erudite in diplomatic policies and this knowledge was used by Agrippina in her governmental transactions.

Claudius' wife, Empress Valeria Messalina, felt that Agrippina's son, Nero was a threat to her son's position and she sent assassins to strangle him while he was enjoying a siesta. The plot was foiled when they encountered, what they thought was a live snake in Nero's bed. It turned out to be only a snakeskin but, it did the trick as they ran in panic.

When Crispus died in 47 A.D., people had thought that Agrippina had poisoned him in order to gain his estate. These were only rumors and not facts and didn't materialize.

When Messalina, Claudius wife died in 48 A.D., he considered remarrying Pallas, one of Caludius's advisers stated that he should marry Agrippina, thereby uniting the Claudian house and imperial family. As stated previously, they were married on New Year's Day in 49 A.D. This marriage was incestuous according to Roman law. Claudius had to persuade a group of senators that this marriage was for the benefit of the public and not for his personal gratification. Agrippina's intent for having this marriage was to gain power so that her son, Nero would be next in line for the emperorship.

Agrippina had eliminated anyone who was a threat to her position. Therefore, she went ahead and had her distant relative Lollia Paulina (a possible wife for Claudius) exiled, accusing her of black magic. Lollia was forced to leave Italy and eventually committed suicide.

Another person whom she became involved with was Silanus, who had been betrothed to Claudius' daughter, Claudia Octavia. She wanted her son, Nero to marry Claudia. Silanus had been falsely charged of having an affair with his sister, Junia Calvina. Silvanus was forced to resign from public office by an interdict from Claudius and he, being despondent, committed suicide. His sister Calvina was exiled from Italy. Then, in 54 A.D., Agrippina had Silanus's eldest brother, Marcus Junius Silanus Torquatus, murdered.

She, also, had Domitia Lepida murdered, Messalina's mother.

Claudius found a Roman colony which was named after his wife, Agrippina, which is known today as Cologne where she was born.

In 50 A.D., she was given the honorary title, Augusta. She was the second living Roman woman to have received this title.

Then, in 51 A.D., she received a carpentum (a ceremonial carriage) which she used very frequently. Agrippina, being the shrewd and cunning manipulator that she was, convinced Claudius to adopt her son, Nero and appoint him as his successor to the crown.

On June 9th, 53 A.D., Nero and Octavia, Claudius's daughter, married. Later, Claudius repented for marrying Agrippina and for adopting her son, Nero, as his successor. He, therefore, prepared his son, Britannicus for the throne. This intent was all that Agrippina needed to eliminate Claudius as emperor.

She went ahead on October 13th, 54 A.D., and poisoned Claudius with a plate of mushrooms at a banquet. Stories have varied as to his cause of death. Some accounts have stated he had died from natural causes.

Agrippina, in the first months of Nero's reign, controlled the empire and her son Nero had an affair with a freedwoman named Claudia Acte. It was at this juncture that she began to lose authority over her son.

Because Agrippina began to support Claudius's son, Britannicus as emperor, Nero had him poisoned during a banquet.

In 55 A.D., she was forced out of the palace by her son. She was released from all power of governing and Nero had Pallas, his adviser, dismissed from the court.

In 57 A.D., having been dismissed from the palace, she was sent to Misenum to live at an estate there.

There have been many stories given as to the cause of Agrippina's death. One such story stated that Nero wanted to marry Poppaea Sabina, a noble woman, but he had to divorce his wife, Octavia, first. He felt that this wasn't feasible with his mother alive so, he decided to kill her.

Another reason for her elimination was her plotting to place Nero's maternal second cousin, Gaius Rubellius Plautus on the throne.

The Roman historian, Tacitus has stated that Nero considered stabbing or poisoning her but, he felt these methods were too cumbersome and, therefore, decided to build a self-sinking boat for her demise.

Another Roman historian, Suetonius stated that Nero was aggravated with his mother because she was too dogmatic and he tried three times to poison her.

After her death, her body was cremated and various people, including the Senate and Roman army, sent him letters of congratulation for having his mother assassinated.

She was given a tomb in Misenum for burial.

Before her death, she had visited astrologers who predicted that her son would become emperor and that he would kill her.

Her reply to the astrologers was: "Let him kill me, provided he become emperor".

DOMITIAN, EMPEROR OF ROME—96 A.D.

DOMITIAN WAS BORN IN ROME on October 24th, 51 A.D., the young son of Vespasian and his wife Flavia Domitilla Major. His older sister was Domitilla the Younger, and his brother was Titus Flavius Vespasianus.

By 66, Domitian's mother and sister died. Domitian's father and brother, at the time, were participating in Germania and Judea commanding Roman armies. The result of their absence meant that Domitian's adolescence was spent in the quiet of loneliness and solitude. Part of his time was taken with his uncle Titus Flavius Sabinus II. In 68 A.D. Vespasian was called upon to lead the Roman army against the rebellious Jewish insurgents with his son, Titus, who was in charge of a legion.

Vespasian had gained a reputable name as a military leader in the invasion of Britain in 43 A.D. Also, his reputation as a politician was enhanced when he became a consul in 51 A.D. He held various positions in the government, as aedile, praetor, and quaestor which aided his reputation. When he became emperor, (he was a member of the Flavian family), "he found the state almost bankrupt. To rectify the problem, he increased taxation—even went to the extent of taxing the disposal of urine."[1]

Regardless of these lucrative positions, poverty had struck the Flavian household during Domitian's childhood. Nevertheless, the Flavians achieved imperial success and favor in the forties. It was at this time that Vespasian became enthroned by having a successful political career.

Vespasian also served as proconsul in Africa under Nero's regime in the year 63 A.D.

Then on June 9th, 68 A.D., the emperor, Nero, committed suicide and with him the Julio-Claudian dynasty came to an end. This resulted

---

[1] Rodgers, Nigel. Ancient Rome. Publisher, Hermes House; London, p. 34

in a civil war, known in history as the Year of the Four Emperors—Galba, Otho, Vitellius, and Vespasian, all renowned generals.

Then, through various encounters between the competing generals for the emperorship, Vespasian was eventually named emperor on July 1st, 69 A.D. After accepting this position, he entered into an alliance with the governor of Syria, Gaius Licinius Mucianus and made war with Vitellius—the Second Battle of Bedriacum which resulted in the defeat of Vitellius. Vitellius sought a treaty with Vespasian but, the Praetorian Guard prevented him from enacting the agreement considering it dishonorable and disgraceful.

On December the 19th, the troops of Vitellius invaded the capital and won a decisive victory. The defender, Sabinus, was captured and executed during the melée. Domitian, however, avoided the onslaught by disguising himself as a worshipper of Isis. Then, in the afternoon of December 20th, Vitellius had died and his armies were defeated.

Domitian was given the title of <u>Caesar</u> which is one of honor and fame.

Besides this award, Domitian became the praetor which involved consular power.

Mucianus, the governor of Syria and ally of Vespasian, ruled in the absence of Vespasian. He curtailed the duties of Domitain who was only 18 years old at the time, making sure he didn't become too ambitious and too powerful. He also made an efficacious effort to see that Domitian didn't become too popular with the military.

After the revolt in Batavia, in which Domitian took part, Mucianus prevented him from participating in further military campaigns. Then, when his father returned to Rome, Domitian devoted his time to literature forfeiting his role in government.

With his political career in jeopardy, Domitian turned his attention to marriage and became attached to Domitia Longina, wife of Lucius Aelius Lamia. Domitian asked Lucius to divorce his wife so that he could marry her. She was the daughter of Gnaeus Domitius Corbulo, a renowned general and a prestigious politician.

In the year 65 A.D., when a conspiracy against Nero failed, Corbulo had been forced to commit suicide because of his involvement in the conspiracy.

Then, in 73 A.D., Domitian's only son died in childhood. Domitia was given the title of <u>Augusta</u> by Domitian and he bestowed on his son, deification.

In 83 A.D., Domitian exiled his wife Domitia for reasons unknown but, soon recalled her. There have been several rumors given why he recalled her—his love for her and his relationship with Julia Flavia, his niece. Roman texts have stated that Domitia lived happily at the palace for the rest of her life despite allegations of divorce and adultery in their marriage.

On September 13th, 81 A.D., Titus, Domitian's older brother and emperor, died of a fever while touring the territories of the Sabine. Domitian's relationship with his elder brother, Titus, wasn't very close because he very rarely had contact with him. Also, little sympathy was shown by Domitian when his brother was dying. Instead of attending his brother's illness, he opted for a journey to the Praetorian Camp where he was proclaimed emperor. Then, on September 14th, the Senate confirmed his appointment and granted him the titles, Pontifex Maximus, Augustus, and Pater Patriae.

Domitian immediately moved the center of government to the imperial court which affected the powers of the Senate. He sincerely believed that one of his chief duties was to guide the people "morally and culturally in every aspect of their daily lives." To do this, he assumed absolute political power. His objective was to elevate the Empire to such a degree as it had been under the rule of Augustus. Thus, he became involved in all the various positions of governmental administration—public morals, and especially, taxation, which was efficiently regulated. Because of his astute requirements and his doggedly perception, the government was run very efficiently and corruption was at a standstill. When handing out public offices, he didn't favor his family members or political favorites in the Senate. On the contrary, he doled out positions to men of the equestrian class. Domitian spent little time in Rome but traveled a great deal to European provinces. He spent at least three years of his reign in Illyricum and Germania where he was involved in military campaigns.

His management of the economy wasn't questionable for, it was balanced and efficient for most of his reign. In public financing, he gained a plus.

When he became emperor, he had the Roman currency boosted on a par with the great Augustus. The silver content of the denarius was increased by 12%. For eleven years, he was able to uphold this standard by employing a fixed taxation policy.

When Domitian took office, the Great Fire of 64 took place along with the fire of 79. Domitian went ahead with a building project the likes of which had not been equaled up to that time. The erection of at least fifty structures took place—a stadium, an odeum, and an extravagant palace on the Palatine Hill (Flavian Palace).

On the military front, Domitian was victorious in his battle with the Chatti in which he conferred upon himself the title of <u>Germanicus</u>. Then, later on, about 77 A.D., Agricola became the Roman governor of Britain. He then decided to invade Caledonia (modern day Scotland). In the summer of 84, Agricola, (father-in-law of the historian Tacitus), faced the troops of Scotland in the Battle of Mons Graupius led by General Calgacus. Despite heavy losses, the Caledonian army escaped the slaughter by hiding in the Highlands, thus preventing Agricola from capturing the entire British island.

Agricola, after having served more than six years as governor of Britain, was recalled by Domitian. The reason given was because Domitian felt that Agricola's victories would have outshone his successes at Germania.

To get rid of him, Domitian offered him the governorship of the province of Africa but, because of either ill health or his personal pride, he refused the offer.

Tacitus and Suetonius, Roman historical writers, speak out about the persecutions toward the end of Domitian's reign. They state that at least twenty senators were executed. Lucius Lamia, Domitia Longina's former husband, and three of Domitian's own family were also executed.

Domitian earned the contempt of his family members and the Senate because he treated them on an equal par with all the ordinary Romans.

This contempt for Domitian existed also among the aristocracy, servants, and court officials.

His assassination took place in the palace on September 18th, 96 A.D., in a conspiracy devised by court officials who were disgruntled over his administration. His chamberlain, Parthenius, was the main instigator of the plot, giving as his chief motive for the conspiracy, the execution of Domitian's secretary, Epaphroditus. A freedman of Parthenius, named Maximus, and a steward, Stephanus, also took part in the plot. Then, pretending to betray the conspiracy, Stephanus was allowed to speak to Domitian and, suddenly attacked him, stabbing the emperor in the groin as he was reading a paper. After the stabbing, Domitian was slain seven times by Clodianus, Maximus, Satur, and a gladiator. His body was cremated by his nurse Phyllis who mingled his ashes with those of his niece, Julia.

Nerva was announced as emperor by the Senate on the same day of the assassination. The Senate finally got rid of Domitian their adversary and rejoiced at his demise. The Senate then passed a decree, <u>damnatio memoriae</u>—his arches were removed, his statues were torn down, his coins were melted, and his name in all public records were erased.

Suetonius, Roman historian, writes that the people of Rome were indifferent to his demise. However, because of his friendly relations with the military and their increase in wages due to Domitian's generosity, the military grieved his loss and wanted him deified immediately. The Praetorian Guard demanded the execution of Domitian's assassins. Nerva, the emperor, refused their demand. After they had taken Nerva hostage from the Imperial Palace, he was forced to accept their demands.

Again, a cruel but competent emperor died a horrible death but his legacy lives on.

CARACALLA, ROMAN EMPEROR—217 A.D.

CARACALLA'S REAL NAME, GIVEN AT his birth, was Lucius Septimius Bassianus and he was connected to the family of Marcus Aurelius. Because he wore a Gallic hooded tunic, he was given the sobriquet, Caracalla which referred to this cloak which became very fashionable due to his dress.

Caracalla was born on April 4th, 188 A.D. at Lugdunum, Gaul which is now called Lyon located in France. His father was Septimius Severus who served as Roman Emperor from 198-211 and was considered very cruel. His mother was Julia Domna.

Edward Gibbon, an historical writer, has pictured him as the "common enemy of mankind." He, also, states that Caracalla "traveled from one province to another so that each could experience his rapine and cruelty."

When his father was traveling to Eboracum (now named York), he suddenly died and Caracalla became co-emperor with his brother Publius Septimius Antoninius Geta. Before he died, Severus told his sons: "Make your soldiers rich and do not bother with anything else."

In December of 211, both rulers began to argue about who should rule and, in the process, Caracalla had Geta, the family of his father-in-law Plautianus and his wife, Fulvia Plautilla, and her brother, murdered. He, also, had Geta's friends persecuted, estimated as many as 20,000.

Caracalla didn't stop here in his executions for, in the five years of his reign, he continued to slaughter anyone who opposed him.

In 213, when he encountered an allied German force, he massacred them unmercifully.

Because he wasn't interested in governing, he relied on his mother, Julia to take over his duties because he was to spend more time with the activities of his troops. This type of action didn't sit well with the citizenry and his popularity diminished considerably.

Then, in 213, a German tribe, the Alamanni revolted in the Agri Decumatis. Caracalla, even though he didn't win a decisive victory, nevertheless, did defeat them in battle. After securing a peace agreement, the Senate showed their appreciation for his effort by honoring him with the magnificent title: <u>Germanicus Maximus</u>.

The following year, he traveled to Alexandria, Egypt where the people, after learning that Caracalla had killed his brother in self-defense, produced a satire which disclaimed this act. Caracalla in a fit of rage because of this mockery, unleashed a savage slaughter of Alexandria's leading citizens who had gathered there to greet him. His troops had a "field day" looting the cities' dwellings.

According to the ancient historian, Cassius Dio, over 20,000 people were slaughtered in the melée.

Caracalla liked the military and to show his appreciation for their efforts, he raised their annual pay and bestowed upon them many other mercenary benefits.

Evidently, he had taken his father's advice to treat the military with "kid gloves."

According to the ancient historian, Herodian, in 216 A.D., Caracalla had the guests of Parthia murdered when he allegedly fooled them by accepting a proposal of marriage. Again, this pointed out the magnitude of his cruelty and brutality. This event has gone down in history as the "Parthian war of Caracalla."

While on his trip to Parthia, he was assassinated by an officer, named Julius Martialis who was his personal bodyguard. This killing occurred while he was caught urinating along a roadside on April 8th, 217 A.D.

According to the historian, Herodian, Martialis' brother had been killed earlier by Caracalla on a trumped up charge and Martialis sought revenge by murdering Caracalla. Another historian, Cassius Dio has stated that Martialis killed Caracalla because he had not been promoted to the position of centurion.

Martialis had slain Caracalla with a dagger at Carrhae in 217. He fled the scene on a horse but, was killed immediately by one of Caracalla's archers.

Macrinus, a Praetorian Guard Prefect replaced Caracalla as the emperor of Rome for a brief period. Some historians believe that he had something to do with the conspiracy.

Despite his cruelty and undaunting character, Caracalla did have some benevolent qualities. His interest in the beauty of Rome and his concern for the freemen cannot be denied.

He is noted for installing the Baths of Caracalla which, even today, are looked upon as one of the colossal remnants of an historic period.

According to historian Cassius Dio, he granted Roman citizenship to the freemen throughout the Empire in order to increase taxation to lighten the depletion of the treasury.

He always considered the welfare of the soldiery as noted above. As an example, he intentionally lowered the silver content of the Roman coins by 25 percent in order to give the troops a pay raise.

These rich qualities cannot be ignored despite his brutality and unconcerned interest in the feelings of the common man.

ELAGABALUS, EMPEROR OF ROME—222 A.D.

ELAGABALUS, WHO ALSO WAS NAMED Marcus Aurelius Antoninus but, born as Varius Avitus Bassianus, has been regarded as the most perverted Roman emperor to have ever been enthroned. His mother was Julia Soaemias and his grandmother, Julia Maesa who was instrumental in getting Elagabalus, only 13 years of age at the time, emperor of Rome by winning the confidence of troops and by convincing them that the boy was the illegitimate son of Caracalla. Also, by donating bribes, it secured his enthronement.

In 218, the Senate confirmed him as the rightful successor of Caracalla and not the Praetorian prefect, Macrinus who feared the family of Elagabalus and had them exiled to their estate at Emesa in Syria.

While there, Julia Maesa arranged a plot to get rid of Macrinus. To do this, she employed Elagabalus' tutor Gannys and her eunuch advisor. His mother, Julia Soaemias emphasized most assuredly that her son was the illegitimate heir of the emperor, Caracalla.

In response to all this hoopla, Macrinus had sent his Praetorian prefect, Ulpuis Julianus with a formidable array of troops to quell the uprising which was taking place at Antioch.

Then, an uncanny result took place. Macrinus' force joined the Elagabalus contingent, and then, in the heat of the battle, they turned on their commanders and slew them. Marcrinus' officer, Julianus was beheaded and it was sent back to the emperor. The Battle of Antioch came to a victorious conclusion for Elagabalus' troops.

After the Battle of Antioch, Macrinus, fearful of his life, fled to Italy. However, he was discovered, despite his disguise, and executed in Cappadocia.

Macrinus, in a furious rage, sent letters to the Senate stating that Elagabalus was insane and not capable of holding the position as emperor. Also, he claimed that Elagabalus was not the illegitimate son of Caracalla.

The Senate took immediate action and declared war on Julia Maesa and her grandson, Elagabalus.

Elagabalus finally assumed the title of emperor without the Senate's approval. This type of action was regarded as a common way of doing things during the third century and was not a problem.

Eventually, after the Senate received letters of reconciliation, they responded by accepting Elagabalus as their emperor, and also, accepted the belief that he was the son of Caracalla. As a final gesture, the Senate, in order to make amends, promoted Julia Maesa and Elagabalus' mother, Julia Soaemias to the rank of Augustae.

Elagabalus' reign turned out to be one of perversion, eccentricity and decadence. His vices were enormous. Some historians claim that he was a transsexual. For, at the ripe old age of 14, he wanted a sex-change operation. Not receiving this change, he was castrated which he desired. Then, with a lover named Zoticus, a male slave, he got married and went on a honeymoon.

His abominations were limitless. He gave lectures to prostitutes on how to perform perverted acts with their guests. He, also, claimed to be the patroness of the prostitutes—an uncanny claim.

He went to the extent of prostituting himself to men on the streets. Records have shown that at one time he entered a brothel, told the prostitutes to leave, and took their place by offering various sexual acts to the customer.

In religious matters, he disregarded Roman traditions and "sexual taboos." He replaced Jupiter, the Roman god, with a new god, <u>Deus Sol Invictus</u>. Members of the government were told to participate in the worship of this deity.

Because of his disregard for the sanctity of marriage, he was married five times. He, also, granted personal favors to his homosexual lovers.

Because of his blatant orgies, he lost popularity with the Senate, the Praetorian Guard and the Roman citizens.

His grandmother, Julia Maesa realizing that he was losing power with the Senate and the soldiery, suggested to him that he should adopt his cousin, Alexander Severus as his heir and son.

After a spell, he realized that naming Alexander as his heir wasn't very practical. Therefore, he planned to have his cousin murdered. However, his plan did not come to fruition and his Guards at the palace turned against him. Soaemias, Elagabalus mother, was killed by the Praetorian Guards who entered the palace. Elagabalus was taken down to a latrine and butchered.

He and his mother's heads were cut off and their naked bodies were dragged through the streets. Elagabalus' body was then thrown into the Tiber River.

After this diabolic act, the soldiery announced Alexander Severus as emperor. Following his death, many of his loyal followers were slain, such as, Hierocles, his chariot driver, and Comazon, commander of the Third Legion. El-Gabal, the sun god was returned to Emesa where Elagabalus was the high priest and his religious decrees were changed.

The life of Elegabalus, an 18 year old emperor, came to an abrupt close. His cruelty and unmerciful slaughter of friends and civilians got him into a great deal of trouble. His debauchery and perversions were enormous and unbelievable. These orgies have left their mark in history and will never be forgotten.

ALEXANDER SEVERUS, ROMAN EMPEROR—235 A.D.

ALEXANDER SEVERUS WAS THE LAST Roman emperor of the Severan dynasty. His full name was Marcus Julius Gessius Bassianus Alexianus and he was born in October, 208. His father was Marcus Julius Gessius Marcianus and his mother was Julia Mamaea. His wife's name was Sallustia Orbiana. His cousin was Elagabalus the 14 year old emperor who was chosen by the Third Gallic Legion and his grandmother was Julia Maesa who was very powerful during Elagabalus' reign.

After Elagabalus and his mother were assassinated in the year 222 A.D., and cast into the Tiber River, Alexander became the emperor of Rome proclaimed by the Praetorian Guards and confirmed by the Senate.

During Alexander's administration, his mother, Julia Mamaea wielded a huge amount of power in the government. She had wise counselors to guide him in his administrative tasks. However, eventually, she became very jealous and stirred up a great deal of resentment among the Praetorian Guards and some of his administrators. The result was a whole host of mutinies throughout the Empire. By being very niggardly in the pay of the army, she alienated them. A praetorian praefect, Ulpian, was executed along with a jurist. The famed ancient historian, Cassius Dio, was forced to retire.

Things were going on rather smoothly in his reign until the Sassanids in the East began to cause trouble which eventually led to war. Nevertheless, he entered Rome victoriously in 233 A.D.

Then, in 234 A.D., trouble brewed when the Germans invaded Gaul. These Germanic tribes had crossed the Rhine River and destroyed the forts there. Alexander immediately organized his troops and crossed the Rhine into Germany.

At this time, he apparently lost favor with his legions as he tried to bribe the German tribes; apparently, he was trying to gain time in order to muster his troops and gain a military advantage.

Herodian, the great Roman historian, has stated: "in their opinion Alexander showed no honorable intention to pursue the war and preferred a life of ease, when he should have marched out to punish the Germans for their previous insolence."

The end result of this untimely diplomacy was the enactment of a new leader among his legions—a soldier who became popular by his exploits and who had elevated himself through the ranks; this soldier was Julius Verus Maximinus who was a Thracian.

Then, after this announcement, Alexander and his mother were assassinated by the 22nd Legion. His death was the beginning of a period of instability and turmoil which has become known in history as the Crisis of the Third Century which reduced the prosperity of the Empire.

Alexander was the last of the Syrian emperors. Under his mother's influence and guidance, the empire took hold, and the conditions of the people were enhanced considerably. He selected important and renowned people in his administration, such as, the great historian, Cassius Dio and the famous jurist, Ulpian who was slain during the mutinies which occurred in Rome during the Crisis Period of the Third Century. This was a period of disorder which lasted for fifty years and consisted of economic chaos, Roman civil wars, and rebellions in the territories of the empire.

Nevertheless, despite all these travesties of the period, Alexander was able to enact several functions which helped to stabilize the economy—the coinage standard was increased; he eliminated the extravagance in the court; he lowered the taxes; he established loan offices for the people at a lower rate of interest; improved the living standards for the legions; and, last but not least, he took immeasurable strides to encourage the classics of art science, and literature.

A black mark on his character was his divorce and exile of his wife, Sallustia Orbiana in the year of 227 A.D. because her father, Seius Sallustius attempted to murder Alexander.

After reigning for a brief period of 13 years, Alexander Severus achieved his goals which brought peace and prosperity to the Roman Empire. It can be truly stated that he had the welfare of the people in mind when he accomplished these great feats.

AURELIAN, EMPEROR
OF ROME—275 A.D.

Lucius Domitius Aurelianus, Roman Emperor, who is known in English as Aurelian, has gone down in history as one of the good emperors because of his initiative qualities. He was able to obtain the power which the Roman Empire had lost in the beginning of the third century. He has been tagged as a successful soldier-emperor. After years of rebellion, he reunited the Empire after constant barbarian invasions and the onslaught of greedy monarchs of Palmyra and Zenobia. He earned the accolades of the Roman populace by regaining the territories of Syria, Spain, Gual, Mesopotamia, and Britain. For all these heroic acts, he has been labeled, "Restorer of the World." Because of these successes, he was able to terminate the "Crisis" of the third century which plagued the Roman Empire.

Aurelian was born to a provincial family which was unknown reputably in a small town named Sirmium located in Serbia.

Termed a great soldier and leader, he participated in several wars which elevated him to the rank of general and a cavalry commander of the army of Emperor Gallienus. At the Battle of Naissus in 268 A.D., his cavalry was able to defeat the powerful Goths.

One historical source has stated that he helped to obtain the emperorship for Claudius II by his involvement in the assassination of the Emperor Gallienus in 268 A.D.

After the death of Claudius, his brother Quintillus became emperor. However, the army didn't accept the approval of the Senate for him as the new emperor. Aurelian, a commander in the army, was more popular and well-liked among the troops, and therefore, they proclaimed him emperor in 270 A.D. in Sirmium, his place of birth. This appointment was confirmed by the Senate after the death of Quintillus.

With this problem corrected, Aurelian now had the time and opportunity to face important problems facing Rome. One such problem was the recovery of its vast territories.

In the following years of 248 A.D. when Philip was the emperor of Rome, the country was in financial trouble because of his expensive ceremonies and a civil war within the realm. Because of these unstable conditions, commerce and agriculture took a downfall. Besides all this turmoil, a huge epidemic swept the country around 250 A.D. causing a great deal of hardship by the loss of manpower for agriculture, and more importantly, for the recruitment of the army.

As a result of all these problems, two entities took place outside the Roman state—Palmyrene Empire and the Gallic Empire. In addition, the emperor was faced with the defense of the Balkans and Italy.

These were some of the adverse problems that Aurelian inherited at the commencement of his rule.

Then, in 270 A.D., Aurelian undertook some of these recurring problems by launching several campaigns in northern Italy against the belligerent Vandals, the Sarmatians, and the Juthungi. After several skirmishes, he was able to oust them from Roman territory. Because of these heroics feats, he was given the elegant title—Germanicus Maximus.

Later, in 271 A.D., he was confronted by the hostile Alamanni as they advanced towards Italy. At the time, Aurelian was in Pannonia trying to control the belligerent Vandals and their withdrawal.

As he entered Italy, his army was ambushed near Placentia. Nevertheless, despite this unsuspecting defeat, he managed to attack the Alamanni and defeated them in the Battle of Fano. Then, at Pavia, he finally invoked the coup de grace.

In order to prevent future attacks by these barbarians, Aurelian had walls built around Rome for protection.

Later, he proceeded to the Balkans where he took on the nefarious Goths and, in the foray he killed their leader, Cannabaudes.

Aurelian decided to invade Asia Minor which he captured with very little resistance but, it didn't include Tyana and Byzantium. The reason why Tyana was not included in the takeover was because he had visioned in a dream, Apollonius, the great 1st century philosopher, had lived there whom he admired and highly respected.

After four horrific years of fighting, he was able to secure these vast territories of the Empire and was capable of rendering their reunification.

Aurelian received many accolades for his accomplishments—restored public buildings, punished public officials and officers of the government for misbehavior and took over the distribution of food among the citizens.

He was most lenient in matters of religion and didn't persecute people who believed in other religions. However, he stationed the Sun god as a main one of the Roman pantheon. His intent was to give all the people of the Empire a single god to worship. Aurelian, however, seemed to believe in the "one god, one empire" approach.

In 274 A.D., Aurelian decided to attack Persia. During this march, he was assassinated by a group of his officers while in Thrace waiting to cross into Asia.

These officers had been misinformed by Aurelian's secretary who told them that they were on the list for execution. Because of their loyalty to the emperor, they did not name his successor but waited for the Senate to decide this important matter.

Aurelian's wife, Ulpia Severina took over the reins of government for a period of six months before the Senate had appointed a new emperor. Then, in 276 A.D., they decided to elect Tacitus.

Because of his early demise, Aurelian didn't have the opportunity to restore the political stability of the Empire which was plagued by civil wars and internal bickering.

However, he left his mark on history by preventing barbarian invasions of the empire and the disunity of the realm. He distinguished himself as a great soldier and leader in battle and was well-liked among his people for his heroic deeds.

THOMAS BECKET, ARCHBISHOP
OF CANTERBURY—1170

It seems ironic that a breach of friendship dissolved in a matter of minutes between Henry II, king of England and Thomas Becket, Chancellor and Archbishop of Canterbury. These two important individuals had been close friends for quite some time—they enjoyed together, such activities, as hunting, various games, and drinking bouts. But, all this came to an abrupt end when Becket's character was transformed from a secular to an ascetic human being.

All this happened when Theobald, Archbishop of Canterbury, recognized his skills and ability, and gave him important missions to Rome. Later, he recommended him to King Henry II when the office of Lord Chancellor was vacant in 1155 which Becket accepted at this time.

When Theobald died in 1162, Becket was appointed by Henry as the Archbishop of Canterbury. Henry had high hopes of changing his relationship with the church by appointing Thomas to this important position. His intention was to shift the balance of power between the Church and state. One thing, which irked him, was the prerogatives of the Roman Catholic judicial system. The Church had its own courts and tried priests of offenses instead of being tried in the secular courts. Therefore, Henry wished to regularize the judicial system and take away some of the Church's privileges. Henry felt that the royal courts shouldn't judge the clergy but, only to see that punishment be inflicted on those found guilty after the ecclesiastical courts had condemned them. This type of involvement goes way back to the medieval period when the feudal lords had put priests on the same level as the common serfs.

Henry tried to crush the reputation of Becket and he discredited him for two months by dividing the bishops in order to win their support against the obstinate and courageous Becket.

Then, at the Council of Clarendon, he tried once more to discredit him. The documents were presented to him to sign but he refused. The king tried again in October, 1164, when he arranged a third council to meet at Northampton. Henry's intent was to present him as a traitor and have him imprisoned.

Thomas refused to face the angry barons on the second floor of the hall, so they were forced to come down to the lower floor to condemn him. Becket was accused of contempt of royal authority and misconduct in the Lord Chancellor's office.

Becket was convicted of these charges and fled to France where he was greeted by King Louis VII who offered him protection.

Becket spent several years at the Cistercian abbey of Pontiny. However, he was forced to move to Sens when Henry threatened the Cistercian order.

Becket used his power of excommunication in Church matters and did so to many of his enemies. The Pope of the Roman Catholic Church at this time was Pope Alexander III. Though he sympathized with Becket, he took a more cautious and diplomatic approach to the situation. He sent legates in 1167 to arbitrate the confrontation between the two.

When Henry heard that the Pope was on the verge of excommunicating him, he changed his attitude toward Becket and allowed him to return to England and resume his position.

When Becket heard that Henry's son was coronated in York in 1170 by the bishops of London and Salisbury and the archbishop of York, he excommunicated all three attendants, as this was definitely a breech of Canterbury's privilege of coronation.

The three bishops "took heels" and fled to Normandy where the king of France was stationed.

When Henry II heard about these unsavory reports about Becket, in a moment of frustration, he yelled out to his knights: "Will no one rid me of this turbulent priest". The knights took him at his word and proceeded to the Cathedral at Canterbury to commit their atrocious act.

After Becket refused their demands to submit to the king's will, they struck him with their swords and killed him.

The faithful in Europe venerated him as a martyr and, in 1173, he was canonized by Pope Alexander III in St Peter's Church in Segni.

Henry feeling remorse for this tragic incident humbled himself by doing public penance at Becket's tomb. Under orders from the pope, he had to walk barefoot in a pilgrim's gown and hair shirt through the streets of Canterbury to Becket's tomb. There, he had to confess to the slaughter and asked for pardon. As he bared his back, the monks at Canterbury took their turns by lashing him seven times each.

Because of the large processions across the London Bridge, a chapel was constructed there dedicated in his honor. Pilgrims began and ended their journeys there. Also, an infirmary was created near the bridge-foot by the Augustinians at St. Mary's Priory which was dedicated to Becket.

The citizens of London adopted him as their son and bestowed upon him the city's co-patron saint along with St. Paul.

Becket's fame as a saint has spread throughout the world and there is a mosaic icon which is still visible in Monreale Cathedral in Sicily. Also, the Sicilian city of Marsala has dedicated a church to St. Thomas Becket.

Not enough can be said of a man who came from ordinary folks and arose to great heights in the Catholic Church. He was born in 1118 in Cheopside, London to Gilbert Becket who was a mercer (a dealer in fabrics), and his mother, Matilda, of Mondeville which is situated near Caen.

At the age of ten, Becket received a wonderful education in civil and canon law at Merton Priory in England. Later, he went overseas to further his education at Bologne, Paris, and Auxerre.

As it was said previously, he was taken into the household of Theobald, Archbishop of Canterbury where he received a huge amount of attention and preparation for his eventual appointments to the vacant positions in the government of Henry II.

He will long be remembered for his courage and determination as a cleric as he stood up for the rights of the Catholic Church against a formidable foe and a previous friend, Henry II, King of England.

EDWARD II, KING OF ENGLAND—1327

EDWARD II BECAME KING OF England after the death of Edward I in 1307. Before his death, Edward I was engaged in several battles with the Scots who were determined to gain their freedom from England. The English had defeated the Scots at Berwick and at Dunbar. Then, William Wallace defeated the English at the Battle of Stirling Bridge. However, Wallace was defeated by the English at the Battle of Falkirk in 1298. Robert the Bruce was enthroned at Scone, near Perth, as King Robert I of Scotland. It was under his reign that the Scots defeated the English at the Battle of Bannockburn and regained its freedom when Edward II was King of England.

Edward gave Piers Gaveston, who has been said to be his lover, the earldom of Cornwall. A baronial committee, who disagreed with Edward's appointment, filed a set of Ordinances which were intended to restrict his power of appointments. They, in turn, demanded Gaveston's immediate removal.

Edward, in compliance with the committee's demands, sent Gaveston abroad temporarily but, soon thereafter, permitted him to return. The embittered barons took notice and executed Gaveston in June 1312.

Because of all this turmoil, Edward soon lost his popularity among the barons. His cousin, Thomas of Lancaster who was the head of the barons, became the ruler of England.

In 1318, Edward renewed his kingdom powers due to the influence of Hugh Despenser the Younger. Because the young Despenser invaded Wales, Lancaster retaliated by fighting the Despensers. However, Lancaster was captured in 1322 and executed after his defeat by Edward.

By 1326, because of his relationship with the Despensers, Edward's popularity had diminished and his wife, Isabella who was humiliated by his effeminate courtship, formed a pact with Roger Mortimer in Paris, France.

His denunciation led to Isabella and Mortimer's invasion of England.

They put the pressure on Edward and he was forced to abdicate and was replaced by his son, Edward III who was only 15 years old at the time. Because of his age, Mortimer took over the reins of government while Edward III looked on.

To make sure that Edward would not seek power, Mortimer had him confined at Kenilworth for a short period of time. Later, two knights, John Maltravers and Thomas de Gournay took over the watch of the young king.

In the meantime, Mortimer and Isabella fearing that Edward the II's supporters would come to his aid, decided to maltreat him. They hoped that he would die from this maltreatment, but to their amazement, he endured their punishment. Eventually, in 1327, he was imprisoned at Berkeley Castle and assassinated in his bed by his captors.

His captors conceived the malicious idea of showing his body to the public. They felt that they could convince the public that he had died a natural death.

Edward III, who was 18 years of age in 1330, arrested Mortimer as the conspirator. He was hung at Tyburn after a short trial. His lover, Isabella retired from public life with the stigma of having her husband killed. She, eventually, succumbed at Hertford on August 23rd, 1358.

Edward II has gone down in history as a cruel, calculated despot who was profoundly possessed with the idea of conquering Scotland at any cost in order to gain fame and fortune.

EDWARD V OF ENGLAND—1483

EDWARD AND HIS BROTHER RICHARD's deaths have been controversial as to how and to whom committed these diabolical acts. Historians have reported several people who might have been involved in their disappearance and murder. The most likely suspect that had the most to gain was Edward's Lord Protector, Richard, the Duke of Gloucester who eventually became King of England and who reigned as King Richard III.

Another suspect who has been mentioned as a possible assassin was Richard's one time friend and ally, Henry Stafford, Duke of Buckingham.

Last person who might have been involved in this dastardly act was Henry Tudor who took the throne of England as Henry VII. He gained notoriety by defeating Richard III in the War of the Roses which was fought on Bosworth Field.

This victory ended on a good note as Henry married Elizabeth of York which united both families and finally ended the conflicts. Also, Henry started the Tudor line.

Edward was born on November 4th, 1470, within Westminster Abbey. His mother was Elizabeth Woodville, who at the time of his birth, was forced here because the Lancastrians, led by Henry, had taken power by removing Edward's father Henry IV from the throne during the War of the Roses (called this because the red rose emblem represented the Lancastrians and the white rose, the Yorkists).

Edward, in June, 1471, gained the title as the Prince of Wales. Then, in 1473, he became the nominal president of the Council of Wales and the Marches. This event took place at the Ludlow Castle on the Welsh Marches.

Edward's growing up was closely supervised and certain conditions were laid out by his father as to when, what, where, and how these conditions were to be handled. To arrange and enforce these conditions, the queen's brother Anthony Earl Rivers was selected. He had established himself as a well-known scholar and, therefore was chosen as the right person to fulfill these obligations.

Edwards's father planned his son's marriage when he was only a child. He contacted Francis II, Duke of Brittany, in 1480, whereby an alliance was drawn up between the two which betrothed his son to the duke's four-year-old heir, Anne. When both became adults, they were to be married. However, this hoped-for prestigious marriage never had a chance to materialize as Edward was murdered at an early age.

When Edward IV died, he had selected his brother Richard as the Protector of his son until he became an adult.

Richard decided to meet with Edward's half-brother, Richard Grey and Earl Rivers on the night of April 29th.

However, the following day, Grey and Rivers and Thomas Vaughan, the king's chamberlain, were arrested and later executed.

Richard, then, took Edward to London where he was confined in the Tower of London. His younger brother, Richard, the duke of York, joined him at the Tower.

It was during this time that Richard, the Duke of Gloucester stepped forth with information that both of Edward IV's children were bastards. Richard had assembled lords and commons to agree with him that Edward IV's marriage had been invalid. On June 22nd, Ralph Shaa had presented evidence in a sermon that Edward IV had already been contracted to marry Lady Eleanor Butler. This evidence substantiated Richard's statement as set forth by the assembly.

The result of all this bickering placed Richard on the throne which was later confirmed by an act of Parliament.

Edward IV's children had vanished and were never heard from again.

As was stated previously, their fate remains unknown and the likely candidates in the assassination have already been scrutinized.

Nothing can be said of Edward V's accomplishments as he was never able to do anything worthwhile because of his brief reign as king. He has been regarded as the shortest-lived monarch in English history.

GIOVANNI (JUAN) BORGIA—1497

During the Middle Ages (collapse of the Roman Empire to Italian Renaissance), a period stifled with chaos and tragedy, murders and assassinations were commonplace. Such was the heyday of the Borgia family of the 1400's.

The history of this family is both intriguing and chaotic. Alexander VI, the pope of Rome at the time, was a dissolute and empire-crazed individual. He secured his election as pope by promises and bribes. His greatest concern, during his pontificate of eleven years, was the accumulation of wealth and fame for his four children—Cesare Borgia being the most notorious of the lot.

Despite his ungodly qualities and, his unfitness to be the pope, the people, evidently, were satisfied in his various states. He was regarded as a capable administrator and a erudite man who delved in the arts. In a time when the Italian despots were vying for power, he was able to hold his own. However, historians have regarded him as the most evil among the popes of Rome.

Juan Borgia was the youngest son of Pope Alexander VI and his brother was the notorious, Cesare.

His mother was Vannozza dei Cattanei of the House of Candia and he was born in Rome. Juan married Maria Enriquez de Luna of Spanish descent. He was made 2nd Duke of Gandia, the Papal Gonfalonier, Grand Constable of Naples, Governor of St. Peters, Duke of Sessa, and General Captain of the papal army in 1496.

When Pedro Luis, his half-brother died in 1488, Cesare, who had been guided to a religious vocation by his father, Pope Alexander VI, hoped to be taken away from his religious vocation and become the heir to the dukedom.

However, he was bypassed by his father who gave the dukedom to Juan, his favorite son.

Cesare's jealousy became apparent when he showed his delighted over Juan's defeat near Bassano in January of 1497.

On June 14th, 1497, Cesare and Juan had supper with their mother and several footmen which included a masked man.

According to reports, this mysterious masked man became very fond of Juan and very close.

After they ate, Juan took off with the masked man on Juan's horse. Accompanied by Cesare, they decided to take a different route than he.

Unfortunately, Juan was never seen again. It had been reported that a Tiber boatman saw a man leading a horse which appeared to be a body laid across the saddle.

Later, they found Juan's body in the Tiber River and his body had been stabbed nine times. His friend, the masked man, had also been slain. There weren't any witnesses to verify the slaying.

There have been various versions given for the assassination. One was that his assassin was Antonio Pico della Mirandola who lived near the Tiber River and whose younger daughter had an "affair" with Juan. To get revenge for this sexual encounter, Antonio had committed this atrocious act.

Another belief involved his brother Cesare. The Romans claimed that he committed the assassination.

However, there has been a great amount of dispute regarding this allegation.

Present day historians feel that this was not the case.

Another belief, and more probable, was that the Orsini or the Sforza families who were enemies of the Borgias, had committed the assassination. The Borgias, on the other hand, were notorious when it came to assassinations as they killed anyone who got in their way on their path to fame and posterity.

Juan left two children when he died—Juan Borja y Enriquez (also known as Juan Borgia), the 3rd Duke of Gandia, and a daughter, Francisca de Jesus Borgia, who became a nun at a convent in Valladolid.

History has recorded another tragedy which had descended upon the Borgia family noted for its nepotism and simony.

WILLIAM THE SILENT—1584

DURING THE 16TH CENTURY EUROPE, assassinations and killings were common as the Catholics and Protestants were at each other's throats in a war of religion. A system of punishment, called the Inquisition, was prevalent in France, Italy, the Holy Roman Empire and later, in Spanish America. The purpose of this organization, which was established in 1233, was to punish heresy within the Catholic Church. The most dreaded form was the Spanish Inquisition set up by Tomas de Torquemata, a Spanish Dominican monk who revived the system in 1483. In 1542, because of the Protestant Reformation, the Roman Inquisition had been established.

Originally, those found guilty of heresy were usually excommunicated. This was pronounced after a religious ceremony, the <u>auto da fe'</u> (act of faith). This act in Spain was a preliminary to punishment which was executed by secular authorities.

The ceremony usually ended with the burning of the victim.

However, it was finally abolished in Spain in 1834 only after it had tried some 60,000 cases of heresy. It has been estimated that Torquemada had condemned about 2,000 of those accused of heresy who were burned at the stake.

The man who openly condemned such cruel practices was William the Silent of the Netherlands, also known as, William of Orange. In the 16th century he opposed the oppressive rule of Philip II of Spain. William, being the enemy of Philip, was accused of heresy by the Spanish Inquisition. Philip and his representatives in the Netherlands, the duke of Alva and the duke of Parma, plotted the assassination of William.

After William announced the Act of Abjuration, which renounced allegiance to the king of Spain, several assassinations were attempted on his life.

A sum of 25,000 crowns was offered to anyone who would kill the prince of the Netherlands. Then, the assassins came forward hoping to receive this earthy sum.

In March, 1582, the first of several assassins stepped forward to commit this ugly act. He was Jean Jaureguy. Carrying a pistol, he went to Antwerp where William resided. While he was there, he was able to get behind William and shot him in the head. After this incident, Jean was killed by William's assistants. However, William survived and finally recovered thanks to the care of his devoted wife, Charlotte. She finally succumbed during this ordeal because of sheer exhaustion and fever.

Again, in 1582, two conspirators plotted to assassinate William and his friend, the Duke of Anjou. However, the plot was discovered and the two were arrested. One of the conspirators was convicted and quartered while the other committed suicide in his cell.

The assassins weren't done yet for, in March of 1583, an ambush attempt on the prince's life was foiled. Because of this scare, William decided to shift his headquarters from Antwerp to Delft.

In April, 1584, a man named Hans Hanszoom of Flushing attempted to assassinate William by using explosives. His heinous deed, however, failed and he was executed.

Later, a religious zealot, Balthasar Gerard of Burgundy attempted the assassination of William. In the presence of Parma (a duke of Spain), he offered to kill William and wanted a small amount of money before he committed the act—a guarantee for his troubles. Parma was doubtful about the youngster's ability to commit this assassination and declined his advancement of money. Nevertheless, Parma did promise him that he would give him the full amount if he succeeded.

Gerard, then, proceeded to Delft where William was housed. He came as a poor Calvinist and asked William for some money. William, feeling sorry for him, gave him 12 crowns.

Instead of leaving the premises, Gerard hid in one of the rooms of the court.

As William entered one of the rooms, Gerard appeared and shot William three times. William died immediately.

Gerard was tortured and put to death after he rejoiced for his evil deed.

Parma kept his word and gave the full amount of money to Gerard's parents.

The Dutch Catholics were happy to see William assassinated as he represented the views of the Protestants in the Netherlands. The Protestants, however, were stunned to hear the news of this atrocious act.

The Catholics called it God's vengeance because the Protestants had killed several priests; and also, several Catholic churches were desecrated. This conflict between the two denominations turned out to be a no win contest in the long run.

The Catholics weren't satisfied with just the execution of Gerard. They had his head shipped off to Cologne where it was displayed as a precious relic. The Catholics in Holland (the Netherlands) sought to have Gerard declared a saint.

William was honored in the Netherlands because of his staunch stance against his arch rival, Philip II of Spain and because he fought for the independence of his country. His bravery, in a time of crises, was extraordinary, and therefore, he will go down in history as a gallant hero.

HENRY III OF FRANCE—1589

HENRY, UNFORTUNATELY, WAS BORN AT a time of discontent, when wars and religious persecutions were prevalent. Also, a period clouded with assassinations. As the king of France, he witnessed killings over religion. His Italian regent mother, Catherine de Medeci, made him a lieutenant-general of the royal armies. He led these forces to victory over the Protestant Huguenots in the Battle of Jarnac, and also, in the Battle of Moncontour. These wars were called the French Wars of Religion. It seems that he, as king, would naturally follow in the footsteps of his elder brothers, Charles IX and Francis II who were constantly at war over religion.

As the Duke of Orleans and Duke of Angouleme in 1560, and also, Duke of Anjou in 1566, he became involved in the plot of the St. Bartholomew's Day Massacre in which thousand of Huguenots were butchered. However, it has been reported that he did not participate in this slaughter.

Henry was the third son of Henry II and Catherine de Medici who cherished him as her most favorite son. She cuddled him in his youth and showered him with affection for most of his life. She called him "Precious Eyes". Henry's elder brother, Charles, disliked him immensely because of his various activities but, most of all, his health.

Henry had a sister named Margot. At the age of nine, he pictured himself as a Protestant and refused to attend Mass. This was his method of rebelling against the established Catholic Church. He, also, tried to change Margot's religion to Protestantism.

Although Henry was very skilled at fencing, he preferred to indulge in reading and the arts which his mother, Catherine had loved due to her residence in Renaissance Italy and her literary background.

His sexual preference has been controversial. Documentary references have stated that he was a homosexual and others say he was bisexual.

Modern historians, however, credit him as having several famous mistresses.

His political opposition, in order to get the French people to dislike him, trumped up adverse propaganda to discredit him by stating his homosexuality.

In foreign affairs, in 1570, there were discussions of marriage between Henry and Queen Elizabeth of England as Elizabeth didn't have any heir if and when she died. However, Elizabeth's consternation was directed at Philip II of Spain who had allegedly accused her of piracy because the galleys of Spain, filled with gold and silver from North America, were being intercepted on the high seas by such competent seamen as Sir Francis Drake and Sir Martin Frobisher of England. For Drake's exploits, he was crowned by Elizabeth who, naturally, denied such invasions of piracy. Nothing was accomplished from these discussions as Elizabeth wasn't interested in marriage at the time; and also, because of their religious differences, she being a Protestant and he a Catholic posed a feeling of friction between the two.

Philip II resorted to name-calling as he labeled her a "public whore". He also, contemptuously referred to her as an "old creature with a sore leg".

Henry's reign expanded worldwide as he became King of the Polish-Lithuanian Commonwealth on condition that he pledge religious tolerance for the Commonwealth.

Anna Jagiellon, who was the sister of King Sigismund II Augustus, played an important part in this transaction as she had urged the parliament of the Commonwealth to elect Henry on the basis that he would have to wed her.

His brother, Charles IX of France died after Henry's coronation as king of the Polish-Lithuanian Commonwealth and he decided to return to France. There, on February 13th, 1575, at the Rheims Cathedral, he was crowned king of France.

In 1576, Henry signed the Edict of Beaulieu which gave the Huguenots many concessions. Because of these transactions, Henry I, Duke of Guise, formed the Catholic League. Henry was later forced to rescind these concessions which he gave to the Huguenots in the Edict of Beaulieu.

Henry was in a constant struggle with the famous House of Guise and Henry of Navarre. It has been reported that Henry took an important part in his mother's conspiracy with the family of Guise to assassinate Admiral Gaspard de Coligny in 1572. This killing had launched the horrific Massacre of St. Bartholomew in which thousands of Huguenots were killed.

Later, because of his diminishing power, Henry, in 1588, became involved in the assassination of the duke of Guise. He invited Guise to participate in a conference and as he entered the council chamber, he was stabbed to death by nine assailants.

Henry wasn't satisfied with this killing as he went ahead and had the duke's brother, Louis, the cardinal of Lorraine, killed.

Because of these vengeful deaths, the Catholics of the Holy League rose up in defiance and drove him from Paris.

In order to try to take back the capital of Paris, Henry was forced to ally himself with Henry of Navarre who used a Huguenot army to do the job.

Then, Parliament accused Henry of the murders and he and Henry of Navarre established a Parliament of Tours.

Then, on August 1st, 1589, while Henry was preparing to attack Paris, a fanatical Dominican friar, Jacques Clement, after learning of Henry's part in the assassinations, became inflamed with passion, especially, when he heard of the sadness of Catherine, the duchess of Montpensier and, the sister of the murdered Guises.

The monk procured a dagger and gained access to the king's chamber stating that he had important secret documents to give him. Granting him privacy, Clement leaned over to whisper the message in Henry's ear. At this juncture, he proceeded to lunge a knife into Henry's stomach.

The following morning Henry III died. This was the day that he had planned an assault to retake Paris.

Henry III was interred at the Saint Denis Basilica. His wife, Louise of Lorraine, did not bear him any children to inherit the throne.

Henry III was the last of the Valois kings. He was succeeded to the throne of France by Henry III of Navarre, the first of the Bourbon kings. Henry III of Navarre is noted for the quote: "Paris is well worth a Mass". In other words—become Catholic and abjure Protestantism in order to secure Paris.

HENRY IV OF FRANCE—1610

HENRY IV, ALSO KNOWN AS Henry III, King of Navarre, was born on December 13th, 1553 at Pau, France. He was the first monarch of the Bourbon family of the Capetian dynasty in France. His father was Antoine the Duke of Vendome and his mother was Jeanne d'Albret, Queen of Navarre. Henry's right to the throne of France was due to his father's connection to King Louis IX, a tenth-generation descendant of the King. When Henry III, King of France died having no son to replace him, Henry IV of Navarre became king. Being a staunched Huguenot, it took several years before the Catholics (majority in France) recognized him as the rightful king.

Henry IV came to power during a time of religious wars between the Catholics and Protestants of Europe. In order to occupy Paris, he had to renounce his faith several times and become a Catholic. In 1572, he did so to save himself from being killed during the St. Bartholomew's Day Massacre of the Huguenots.

Later, he returned to the Protestant faith, then, he had to abjure his faith a second time before he could enter Paris which was controlled by the Catholic League forces.

In 1593, he finally entered Paris stating: "Paris is well worth a Mass".

Up to this time, Henry, even after he had defeated the Catholic League at Arques and at Ivry, was prevented from entering Paris, the capitol city of France. Thanks too, with the support from Spain and the Virgin Queen of England, Elizabeth who supplied money and troops, he was able to win these victories and his kingdom by military conquests.

Henry's first marriage to Margaret of Valois, daughter of Henry II and Catherine of Medici, wasn't a happy one and a childless marriage. Their wedding took place in Paris at the Notre Dame Cathedral on August 19th,

1572. Even before Henry IV had been enthroned as king of France, his wife, Margaret, separated from him and went to live at Auvergne in a beautiful chateau of Usson.

Needing an heir to the throne, Henry contemplated an annulment of his marriage to Margaret. He became very fond of Gabrielle d'Estrées who had already borne three children to him and who wanted to marry her.

However, Henry's councilors were definitely against this idea. This matter was resolved, when on April 10th, 1599, Gabrielle suddenly died due to the stillborn death of her son to whom she had given birth prematurely.

Later, Henry married Marie of Medici in 1600 after his marriage to Margaret was annulled in 1599.

Henry became one of the most popular rulers in France due to his concern for his subjects. He lightened the burden of taxation on his people and provided the necessary foods to sustain life. His interest in the peasant farmer and industrial worker knew no bounds. This egalitarian king brought prosperity and peace to a nation grounded in religious turmoil. His charisma outshone the lives of other kings of France and his performance was enhanced by a loyal minister, Maximilien of Bethune, the duke of Sully, who promoted agriculture, education, and stabilized the government's financing; also, had swamps drained to increase the production of agricultural crops. He and the competent Maximilien constructed canals and bridges and built tree-lined roads. To beautify the countryside and parks, Henry was engaged in the planting of various trees—elms, pines and fruit. He also had constructed the Pont Neuf which connects both banks of the Seine River. In addition, Henry had the Place des Vosges built and had the Grande Galerie attached to the Louvre.

Henry was also interested in the expansion of France and in foreign trade so, he financed several expeditions to North America. Brave men, such as Samuel Champlain, Sieur of Monts, and Pierre Dugua participated in these ventures. One benevolent result was the claiming of Canada which increased France's wealth by her stance in the fur trade. France also formed a company in 1600 with Laval and Vitré through the Saint-Malo association which opened up routes to Japan and the Moluccas. Francois Martin of Vitré had reached Ceylon and set up trade in Sumatra but was later taken prisoner by the Dutch on his return at Cape Finisterre. He was asked by Henry to write about his travels to the Far East.

Because of Vitré's travels to Asia, Henry acquired a profound interest in this part of the world and proceeded to form the French East India Company.

In 1604, his interest in adventure extended to a contact with merchants of Dieppe and asking them to form a Dieppe Company. He gave them exclusive rights for 15 years to trade in Asia.

Then, in 1609, Pierre-Olivier Malherbe had a conference with Henry in which he related his adventure of circumnavigation and his visit to China and his meeting with Akbar, ruler of India.

France, at the time, wasn't on friendly terms with Spain and the Hapsburg dynasty. The French Huguenots allied themselves with the Moriscos of Aragon and planned a combined assault against Spanish Aragon. However, this plan of attack was foiled with the arrival of John of Austria in Aragon.

In 1576, an Ottoman fleet of ships were employed to disembark around Valencia, Spain while the French Huguenots and the Moriscos would invade Hapsburg, Spain. However, this operation wasn't accomplished because the Ottoman fleet failed to arrive. Nevertheless, Henry continued the alliance with the Ottoman Empire and in 1601 he received an embassy from Mehmed III.

Then, in 1604, a peace treaty was signed between Henry and Ahmet I of Turkey which gave a whole host of advantages to France.

Even though he served his people well, there were others who hated him for his affiliation with the Catholic Church.

Several attempts were made on his life. In August of 1593, Pierre Barriere attempted to assassinate him and in December, of 1594, Jean Chatel also tried to kill him.

Then, on May 14th, 1610, the tragedy took place in Paris. While he was on his way to visit the Duke of Sully, who was ill at the time, a fanatic, Francois Ravaillac of Angouleme entered the coach carrying Henry and thrust a dagger above Henry's heart which cut his aorta while Henry was reading a dispatch. Ravaillac had been arrested previously for a crime he didn't commit. While he was incarcerated, he claims to have had a vision in which he was to save France from Protestantism.

Henry was buried at the Saint Denis Basilica. Marie of Medici, his widow, became Regent because her son, Louis XIII was only nine years old.

Henry, a gentle, compassionate king who loved his people was honored for years. Because of his popularity, a statue was constructed in 1614 at the Pont Neuf just four years after his death.

Again, a great king died before his time but, was highly honored for his outstanding accomplishment when he lived.

SHAKA—1828

ONE MAY ASK WHY THIS author selected a Zula chieftain to write about. The answer is simple. When writing about the Battle of Isandlwana of 1879 between the British and the Zula armies, the British suffered a severe beating. This author came across the name of this remarkable and vigorous chieftain whom I had described about his magnificent feats in my book—<u>World Battles and Their Leaders Who Changed Global History</u>.

He has been regarded as a military genius because of his innovations in changing military tactics and instruments of warfare for his Zula army. On the other hand, he has been condemned for the brutality he inflicted on his enemies and his own people during his reign.

The deaths he caused in his ten-year kingship are enormous. He executed and disrupted tribes. They migrated because of the fear and brutality of his Zula army.

Shaka, during his reign, ruled some 250,000 people and developed a formidable army of about 50,000 warriors.

His triumphs were innumerable as he raided, invaded, and conquered other tribes.

Shaka had recognized Dingiswayo, who was the leader of the Mthethwa clan, as his overlord.

Dingiswayo was killed in a ambush by Zwide's Ndwandwe and Shaka was able to form an alliance with the Mthethwa clan, and also, gained support among the Qwabe after their leader, Phokathwayo, was overthrown. With these various tribes, Shaka organized a formidable force of clans which was able to confront the Ndwandwe in battle—the Battle of Gqokli Hill in which he emerged the victor.

Later, Shaka traveled some seventy miles to the royal kraal (a South African native village) of Zwide, ruler of the Ndwandwe, and completely obliterated it. Zwide was able to escape this onslaught but, died later on, the cause of his death unknown.

As it was stated previously, Shaka was a military genius and all his victories didn't come about haphazardly but, were designed with the utmost perfection.

As stated, they can be attributed to his innovations of tactical warfare and his design of new weapons. He was dissatisfied with the long throwing assegai (long spear) and developed the Iklwa, a short stabbing spear. He, also, was instrumental in the development of a large shield which was made of cowhide.

The stabbing spear was used in hand to hand combat while the throwing spear was used before close combat took place.

Another of his innovations was his constant drill and forced marches to get his army in top-notch condition. He, also, did away with the foot-sandal in order to increase greater mobility in contacting the enemy.

Those militants who refused to go without the sandals were killed without any hesitation on his part.

Some of his forced marches were made at a fast trot and covered more then fifty miles. He was noted for drilling his troops in encirclement tactics. This tactic was used quite cleverly during the Isandlwana battle with the British in 1879 in their defeat.

Shaka was responsible for organizing regiments based on age groups and placed them in special military kraals.

These age groups were given a variety of duties, such as, the herding of cattle, guarding a camp, and participating in certain ceremonies and rituals.

These youth formations were adapted for providing logistical support for the army. Their ages ranged from six years and older and they were apprentice warriors. They were used for various details, such as, carrying supplies, such as, cooking pots and rations for the troops. They, also, had to carry extra weapons for the soldiers and their sleeping mats. These duties were used primarily in support of very light forces when capturing towns and pillaging neighborhoods.

Another unique formation, which Shaka has been given credit, was the "buffalo horns". This formation was composed of three divisions: First, there was the "chest" (the main force) which contacted the enemy (Impi) and kept it in position. Second, the "horns" would then flank the Impi from both sides and encircle it while the "chest" had pinned the enemy down. Third, the "loins", which consisted of a huge amount of reserves, was situated behind the "chest" with their backs to the battle and whose responsibility it was to come to the aid of the "chest" if and when the Impi had broken out of the encirclement.

These units were coordinated by leaders (chiefs) who used messengers and hand signals where appropriate, to supply the necessary relief to achieve their goals.

Any grouping of men assigned on a mission could be named an Impi (warrior or enemy) and were organized into three groups: regiments, corps (composed of several regiments), and armies. These groups were not uniform in numbers but depended on the king's orders or sometimes mustered by localities or chiefs of various clans. The corps usually took their name from the military kraals from which they came.

Shaka's early life is one of intrigue and ambiguity. He was probably the first son of the chieftain Senzangakhona and Nandi, a daughter of Bhebhe, the past chief of the Langeni tribe. He was conceived out of wedlock. Several reports have stated that he was disowned by his father, Tabile Raziya and driven into exile. Other reports have stated that his parent's marriage was legitimate.

As a child, his mother took very good care of him and there developed a close relationship between the two.

In his early days, Shaka became a warrior under the aegis of the local chieftain, Dingiswayo. Dingiswayo made Shaka a member of an age group by which he was included in the Izichwe regiment. For a period of ten years, Shaka served as an Mthethwa warrior.

When Dingiswayo was murdered by Zwide, a powerful chief of the Ndwandwe clan, Shaka wanted revenge for his close friend's murder and began to pursue Zwide who barely escaped his grasp. However, Shaka was able to capture Zwide's mother, Ntombazi, and had her killed by locking her in a house with hyenas which devoured her. After this gruesome act, Shaka had the house burned to the ground.

It was not until 1825 that Shaka caught up with Zwide at the border of Kwa Zulu-Natal where Shaka was victorious.

At this time, Shaka established his capital, Bulawayo in Qwabe. It was here that Nqetho ruled as a proxy chieftain for Shaka.

Shaka's domination was based primarily on military might. However, he used patronage and diplomacy to win over friendly chieftains. Shaka's mother and his wife Nandi were important people in his life. He had no offspring even though he had 1,200 women at his harem. Those concubines who became pregnant were disposed of by execution.

His behavior changed drastically when his wife Nandi and his mother died in 1827. At this time he became psychotic and did some bizarre things. While he was in mourning, he had 7,000 Zulus killed or sacrificed. For a year he did not permit crops to be planted and no milk to be used. Any woman who became pregnant was killed along with her husband.

At this time, he went on a rampage and had his army take territory all the way to Cape Colony. He then ordered his forces to proceed north to take more territory.

The troops finally rose up in anger because of their harsh treatment. A party of plotters, headed by two of Shaka's half-brothers, Dingane and Mhlangana, stabbed him to death on September 22nd, 1828. Then, Dingane took over the reins of government.

Dingane was accosted by European Voortrekkers from the Cape right after Shaka's death. The Voortrekkers recovered from an attack by the Zulus and dealt the Zulus a major defeat at the Battle of Blood River.

As was stated previously, the Zulus won an outstanding victory over the British at the Battle of Isandlwana in 1879. The Zulus also forced back a British column at the Battle of Hlobane Mountain using a fast-moving regiment, a tactic employed earlier by Shaka during his reign.

There is a tendency is to lionize Shaka and the media did built up his appeal worldwide. However, one must consider the destruction, the devastation, and the massacres of some 2 million dead when forming a favorable opinion of him.

ABRAHAM LINCOLN—1865

IN MY PERSONAL OPINION, I feel as many scholars do, that Abraham Lincoln has gone down in history as one of our greatest presidents. When we look at him in various pictures, we see a man who had undergone various tragedies in his life, beginning with the death of his younger brother Thomas who died in infancy at the age of nine and also, losing his mother to a disease called "milk sickness." Besides these deaths his sister, Sarah, died during childbirth at age 21. Then, later in life, we see a gaunt, tiresome look on a president during the Civil War in which thousands of soldiers lost their lives fighting for a cause they thoroughly believed in—freedom of slavery and civil rights to a minority race.

Despite his despondency, he was a man with a purpose who persevered in the light of tragedy and chaos.

Lincoln came from a poor family—his father was Thomas Lincoln and his mother was Nancy Hanks and they lived in a log cabin near Hodgenville, Kentucky where "Abe" was born in February 12th, 1809.

When he was nineteen years old, he was carrying produce down the Mississippi and Ohio Rivers to New Orleans on a flatboat.

In 1830, in Decatur, Illinois he worked splitting rails for fencing. Later, he left home and worked at various jobs. He was a storekeeper in the village of New Salem, Illinois.

Lincoln had little education. He had attended school for a brief period in Kentucky. Most of his education was achieved by his own labor. He would read constantly under candle-light in the evenings, both classical books and school primers.

During his studies he took a profound interest in the writings of Robert Burns and the 16th century writer, William Shakespeare.

Later, he was asked by the governor of Illinois to lead a group of volunteers to quell a rebellion by the Fox and Sauk Indian tribes who were forced to leave Illinois.

Lincoln decided in 1834 to enter the political arena and was elected to the Illinois State Legislature. In 1837, he became a lawyer and was elected to the United States House of Representatives in 1846 where he served one term.

Returning to Springfield, Illinois, he began putting his knowledge of law into practice.

Lincoln became involved in a series of debates with Stephen Douglas who was regarded as a noted orator and a shrewd and outspoken senator. The issue under discussion was Douglas' view about slavery being legalized in new territories that became states. He had put forth his famous Kansas-Nebraska Act which would have repealed the Missouri Compromise that limited slavery to only those states where it had existed in 1820.

Lincoln, who was an ardent critic over the slavery question, argued most vehemently about the tenets of this proposal as espoused by Douglas.

Lincoln became nationally renouned for his brilliant oratory in these debates which projected him as a presidential candidate of the newly formed Republican Party.

Because of his stance against slavery in general, he was threatened by South Caroline of secession if and when Lincoln should become president of the United States. As it might have been expected, because of Lincoln's popularity, he was heaved into the lime-light and was chosen as the 16th President of the United States in 1860.

South Carolina immediately began a movement of secession followed by eleven more Southern states. This group of states formed the Confederate States of America and elected Jefferson Davis as its president.

Lincoln vowed to go to war, if necessary, to preserve the Union. However, it was the Confederacy which took the "first step" and attacked the United States Army post at Fort Sumter on April 12th, 1861, which was under the command of Major Robert Anderson who had to eventually surrender the fort as he had run out of supplies and ammunition.

Thus, the Civil War had begun and before it was over 600,000 men lost their lives. This holocaust could have been averted if the South had agreed to free their slaves. But this could not be, the agricultural South depended on slave labor as a means of wealth and livelihood.

It was during this bloodshed that Lincoln issued his famous Proclamation Emancipation in which he gained the elegant sobriquet the "Great Emancipator."

The first battle occurred at Bull Run on July 21st, 1861, where the Confederacy gained an overwhelming victory.

However, as the war progressed, the Union achieved major victories. One was at Gettysburg, Pennsylvania where Lee attempted to invade the North and cut off Union supplies; also, at Antietam, one of the bloodiest battles of the war; and, at Vicksburg, Mississippi.

The battle at Vicksburg, Mississippi was accomplished when General Ulysses S. Grant took this important stronghold which split the South in two. Credit has to be given to the great General Winfield Scott whose Anaconda Plan was put into operation by the command of Lincoln.

Scott was a wise, military commander and strategist who had written a book titled: <u>Infantry Tactics</u> which was the first complete manual of military strategy for the Army of the United States.

When Lincoln realized that General George B. McClellan was too cautious and hesitant in pursuing the enemy, he released him from his duty as the commander of the Northern Army of the Potomac. Lincoln tried several generals for this post—Scott, Ambrose Burnside, George G. Meade, and Joseph Hooker.

Finally, disgusted with the failures of these commanders, he stated: "I want a general who fights." That man for the job was Grant, a pugnacious, bold, and at times an arrogant militant.

Accompanied him was another great General, William Tecumseh Sherman noted for his famous march through Georgia and into Carolina employing his tactic of attrition. After the war, he became commander of the Army of the United States taking over the command from Ulysses S. Grant who was the first commander to hold that rank since George Washington did during the American Revolution of 1775.

The war finally came to a climax with the surrender of Robert E. Lee when Grant took Richmond, capital of the Confederacy. Lee surrendered to Grant on April 9th, 1865 at the Appomattox Courthouse in Virginia.

After the war Jefferson Davis went to Canada where he was hired by an insurance company. Davis, eventually, returned to the United States when President Andrew Johnson issued a full pardon to the Confederate leadership. This act of clemency occurred on Christmas Day in 1868.

Davis's final days of life were spent in Mississippi. His final words were spoken to a reporter in which he stated: "that I only loved America."

After Lincoln signed a pardon of a boy-deserter and pardoned a Confederate spy, he and his wife took a carriage ride which he felt would relieve him of the burdens he faced while executing the Civil War.

On April 14, 1865, Lincoln and his wife, Mary, went to Ford's Theater to see the play, Our American Cousin. This trip was taken as a means of relaxation from the burdens of administration which Lincoln was facing during this trying period. While Lincoln was enjoying the play, John Wilkes Booth, a prominent actor, entered the booth where Lincoln was seated.

A security guard had left his post and Booth entered the chamber undetected. With a small brass derringer in his grasp, Booth fired a shot which penetrated the President's temple. Major Rathbone who was also seated in the box attacked Booth who had a knife. Booth leaning against the railing of the box managed to free himself from the grasp of Rathbone and vaulted down to the stage. However, Booth's boot spur got caught in a flag on his descent and as he hit the stage, he broke his leg.

When he contacted the stage, he uttered: "Sic semper tyrannis" ("Thus always to tyrants," the motto of Virginia).

He escaped out of the theatre but was later captured in a barn. He died of gunshot wounds—said to be inflicted upon himself.

Today, we remember Lincoln mainly for his eloquent Gettysburg Address in which he addressed his desire to preserve the Union at all costs and to end slavery which he regarded as immoral.

His Gettysburg address of 1863 will never be forgotten. His speech is regarded as the greatest in American history. His famous words still ring out, loud and clear: "this nation, under God, shall have a new birth of freedom, and that government of the people, by the people, for the people, shall not perish from the earth."

ALEXANDER II, CZAR OF RUSSIA—1881

ALEXANDER II WAS BORN ON April 29ᵗʰ, 1818, in Moscow. He was the
eldest son of Nicholas I of Russia and Charlotte of Prussia. He was also
the Grand Duke of Finland and the King of Poland. At age 37, he acceded
to the throne upon the death of his father in 1855 and became known as
Alexander the Liberator.

Feeling the pulse of the Russian people after Russia's defeat in the
Crimean War, he began a period of radical reforms—a development
of Russia's natural resources and, a reformation of all branches of the
administration. His bravery in governmental matters was shown in a
period when changes in St Petersburg were at a standstill and unfavorable
to the aristocracy. Also freedom of thought and criticism of the upper
classes were thoroughly suppressed.

His education was limited to a certain degree as he received a smattering
of literary subjects and several modern European languages. He was
schooled in this subject matter by the romantic poet, Vasily Zhukovsky.

To open up his horizons in world affairs, he was taken on a six-month
tour in Russia where he visited several provinces. Later, to enlighten his mind
in the realm of political affairs, he toured several western European countries.

When peace was restored after the Crimean War, Alexander began to impose
certain changes in legislation which involved industry and commerce.

A network of railways took place which helped to develop the natural
resources and provided for the defense of the country from attack by
belligerents.

Most important, the question of serfdom was attacked headlong and
he authorized committees to investigate the conditions of the peasants.
Taking a hint from the Lithuanian government in their transactions with
the landed proprietors in their dealings with the serfs, they were very

generous and patriotic. Alexander felt that this amelioration of generosity would rub off in the Russian provinces.

He was right in his thinking as emancipation committees were formed in all the provinces where serfdom existed.

Alexander had to solve this question of serfdom which was plaguing his government and his personal well-being.

He finally consented to their liberation and his brother, Konstantin took the reins of emancipation into his own hands and transacted the necessary manifesto. It took six years after his accession to the throne when the emancipation law took effect and was published and signed.

Alexander was also noted for other important reforms which helped to strengthen his government. Taking a lesson from Russia's defeat in the Crimean War, he realized that immediate steps had to be taken to strengthen Russia's defenses. Therefore, he initiated a program whereby the military, army and navy rearmament and reorganization, was introduced. Changes were made which included an army reserve, a military district system, military education of officers, and universal military conscription.

Besides the transformation of the military apparatus, he set his eyes on the judicial system. Here, he changed the civil and criminal procedure to make it more workable and devised a new penal code.

He had elective assemblies who were given the power to tax the populace in rural and large towns and gave the Minister of the Interior the power to select municipal police in these towns.

Alexander's sex life dazzled the imagination. He had an insatiable appetite for women. Besides having six sons and two daughters by his wife Marie, he also fathered seven known illegitimate children. After his wife had died on June 8th, 1880, he married his mistress Princess Catherine Dolgorukov with whom he already had four children.

Alexander, as king of Poland, restricted their government's position in Lithuania, Belarus, Livonia, and Western Ukraine. This strapping of political freedom caused the January Uprising of 1863-1864. This uprising was finally suppressed by Russia after eighteen months of warfare. The result of this conflict was horrendous. Thousands of Poles were deported to Siberia and hundreds were executed.

Alexander clamped down on the policies affecting Poland-Lithuania. He had all the territories of these two nations excluded from liberal policies. For instance, the martial law in Lithuania lasted for the next forty years which had been enacted in 1863.

Alexander had the Polish language banned in all provinces which encompassed both oral and written form.

In Finland, he made his mark by establishing a good relationship with the people there. He accomplished this act by elevating the Finnish language on a national level instead of local vernaculars.

Because of these reforms, Alexander gained the sobriquet, "The Good Czar" in Finland.

Nevertheless, there were still unhappy people in Russia who were determined to get rid of this autocrat.

Several attempts were made on his life. In 1866, in St. Petersburg, Dmitry Karakozov attempted to assassinate him. Then, on April 20th, 1879, as Alexander was walking towards the Square of the Guards Staff, he was confronted by Alexander Soloviev who was carrying a revolver. Fortunately, Alexander saw this weapon in his hand and fled the scene. Soloviev fired his gun five times but to no avail. He was captured and hanged.

In December of 1879, the Narodnaya Volya (Will of the People), attempted to assassinate Alexander by putting an explosive on a railway. The first trap was organized by Andrei Zhelyabov, a leader of the People's Will party who had won a scholarship to the University of Odessa. Fortunately for Alexander, the explosive failed to detonate.

On February 5th, 1880, Stephan Khalturin set off a charge under the dining room of the Winter Palace. Again, Alexander "lucked out" as he was late for dinner and missed the bombing. Eleven people were killed in the blast.

A girl named Sophia Perovskaya, a fierce activist, was engaged in another attempt to assassinate the Czar. After learning that there would be two trains on the track, the first to test the safety of the rails and the second to carry the Czar, she and her assailants let the first train pass and derailed the second. However, they were outwitted. The second train was a decoy and the Czar had been placed on the first one.

Then in March, 1881, the route of the royal family was plotted. The plotters had tunneled under the Malaya Sadovaya Street and planted bombs to blow up the Czar's carriage. Four men were assigned as backups if the explosion of the carriage didn't work. However, Zhelyabov was taken by the police and Perovskaya took charge of the plan.

The Czar's security guards, learning of the plan, altered his expected route. The backup killers were now trusted with the assassination because the explosions of the mined-street plan had failed.

It was at this time of events that a 19 year-old student named Nikolai Rysakov was carrying a small white package wrapped in a handkerchief. He threw a bomb that only damaged the bulletproof carriage. The Czar was unhurt but shaken. Rysakov was captured and taken away by the police.

Then, a second assassin, Ignaty Grenevitsky hurled a nitroglycerine bomb which landed at the Czar's feet. The explosion shattered the Czar's legs and blew out an eye. The Czar died within an hour with his family close by. He had been escorted to the Winter Palace at the time of his death.

The assassination caused a backslide for his reform movement.

First of all, an elected parliament, or Duma, that he had planned, fell apart when his son, Alexander III became the Czar.

Second, anti-Jewish pogroms took place because the Jews were said to be involved in the assassination—only one Jew had taken part, however.

Third, there was a suppression of civil liberties in Russia and the police used brutal methods to quell any protesters.

Alexander II will be remembered as a ruler who believed in radical reform to bring about changes in the Russian government despite the opposition of the landed aristocracy who were against his liberation policy concerning the serfs.

JAMES A. GARFIELD—1881

JAMES ABRAM GARFIELD WHO WAS the 20th President of the United States came from a rural, poverty-stricken family. He was born in a log cabin on November 19th, 1831 which was situated in Orange, Cuyahoga County, Ohio. He was of English and French Huguenot ancestry. His father was a farmer who came from Worcester, New York and became famous as a champion wrestler. James was only 18 months old when his father succumbed to a common cold while attempting to quash a forest fire.

His mother was Eliza Ballou Garfield who came from New Hampshire. She was a steady influence on James's successful career and married again, to Alfred Belden after her first husband's death.

However, the marriage didn't last long for he divorced her for desertion.

She, being a healthy woman, outlived her son by nearly seven years. She has been claimed to be the first mother of a president to be able to attend her son's inauguration.

James was the youngest of four children. He had a brother and two sisters.

James received his education in the school district of Orange Township, Ohio. Later, as he grew older, he attended Geauga Academy at Chester, Ohio. Because of financial difficulty, he had to see his way through school by doing odd jobs, such as teaching and carpentry work.

In 1851, he attended the Eclectic Institute located at Hiram, Ohio. Again, to pay his way through school, he was forced to work as a teacher in the schools of Blue Rock and Warrensville, Ohio. He was, also, employed as a janitor there.

His education really took hold when he entered Williams College in Williamstown, Massachusetts.

It was here that he developed a fine reputation as the school's debater. He, also, engaged in several extracurricular activities—president of the Mills Theological Society and the Philologian Society.

While at Williams College, he had spoken several times to the community of Disciples at Poestenkill, New York. In 1850, he became one of the Disciples of Christ.

Then, in 1849, he had a romantic affair with Lucretia Rudolph of Hiram, Ohio. She met James when they were classmates at Geauga Seminary in Chester, Ohio. She was an intellectual and James took an immediate liking of her. They were married at the home of the bride's parents in Hiram, Ohio on November 11th, 1858. They had four sons and a daughter who lived to maturity.

When James died, she lived comfortably on a $350,000 trust fund which was instigated by Cyrus W. Field, her financier.

She was buried at the Lake View Cemetery in Cleveland, Ohio, next to James.

James participated in the American Civil War from 1861 to 1863. He was the commander of the Eighteenth Brigade in the battle of Middle Creek in January 1862 in which he defeated a superior force of Confederates under General Humphrey Marshall. He was promoted to brigadier general for checking the rebel advance into eastern Kentucky.

After the battle of Shiloh of 1862, he contracted a fever which forced him to rest at Hiram, Ohio.

Later, in the battle of Chickamauga in September of 1863, he was promoted by Major General William S. Rosecrans to the rank of major general for his heroics, when under enemy fire, he delivered vital information to Union flanks.

It was during this time that Garfield was elected to Congress and resigned his commission in 1863 to take his position there.

As a noteworthy politician, Garfield rose to tremendous heights in this brief stay in this capacity.

He became a state senator in 1859 and in 1863 a United States Representative. As a state senator, he looked upon the anti-slavery abolitionist, John Brown, as a hero, but did not condone his bloody killings. He also campaigned for Lincoln as president in 1860.

As was mentioned earlier, he was still in uniform when he was elected in 1862 as United States Representative to Congress as a staunch Republican. In this capacity, he sponsored a draft bill and criticized Lincoln for not putting enough energy in dealing with the war. He even went so far as to suggest the execution or exile of the Confederate top brass and confiscation of the rebel's property.

After the war he settled down and showed his leniency toward the South by calling for a just and temperate Reconstruction program which President Andrew Johnson had suggested. However, in the long run, he sided with the Radical Republicans and voted for Johnson's impeachment.

In 1868 and 1872, he went all out in support of Ulysses S. Grant for president of the United States. It was during Grant's administration that Garfield held various important posts—chairman of the Appropriations Committee, chairman of the Banking and Currency Committee, and also, a member of the Ways and Means Committee.

On the tariff issue, he took a middle stand, stated: "I am for a protection which leads to ultimate free trade . . ."

In 1870, he was against handing out federal funds to relieve projects which were taking place during the depression of that year.

Then, in 1873, Garfield was implicated in the so-called Credit Mobilier scandal. He was accused of accepting shares of this Company and a $300 loan. Of course, he denied of any wrongdoing. During a congressional investigation, he testified that he turned down the offer to purchase the stock. However, he did admit of having accepted the loan but stated that he had repaid the loan.

Regardless of the scandal, he won the reelection though his popularity at home diminished considerably.

In 1876, he supported Rutherford B. Hayes for president of the United States while serving on the electoral commission which decided the disputed election in Hayes' favor. During the Hayes administration, Garfield served as the minority leader of the Republican Party in the House of Representatives.

Then, in the 1880 election for United States Senator, because of his nomination for president of the United States, he declined his seat.

In the 1880 election for the presidency, Grant sought a third term as president pitted against James G. Blaine of Maine and John Sherman of Ohio, who were the candidates of the Half Breeds, the Republican moderates.

After the voting took place in Chicago, Garfield was stunned by the voting results as the final votes tallied were 399 for him while the former president, Grant, received 306. In order to placate the Stalwart party, the Republicans nominated Chester A. Arthur of New York as vice president.

It had been said that because of boss Roscoe Conkling of New York's active support of Garfield in the election due to an agreement posed by Garfield in which he agreed to consult with Conkling's subordinates on patronage for the state, he won a decisive victory for the presidency. The meeting was comically dubbed the Treaty of Fifth Avenue.

Conkling interfered with Garfield's appointment of William H. Robertson as collector of the Port of New York. He tried to prevent the confirmation in the Senate to no avail. This defeat broke Conkling's grip on the party and ended his famous or "infamous" career.

During Garfield's first week of the presidency, a scandal arouse titled "Star Route" which involved fraudulent mail route contracts. Garfield ordered an immediate investigation of the charges by Postmaster General, Thomas L. James. It was found that Second Assistant Postmaster General, Thomas Brady, Republican Senator, Stephen W. Dorsey, and others were involved in the scheme. It was estimated that this scheme cost taxpayers around $4 million.

Unfortunately, no one was convicted. The good news, however, resulted in wide civil service reform in government's service contracts.

The real bad news came on July 2nd, 1881, when a disappointed office seeker by the name of Charles J. Guiteau shot the President at the Baltimore and Potomac Railroad Station where he was planning his way to his alma mater, Williams College in Massachusetts. Guiteau, with a British-made Bulldog revolver, fired two shots into Garfield's back.

After he was shot, the President was removed to the White House under the supervision and care of Dr. D.W. Bliss. He was assisted by a group of surgeons. These surgeons performed three operations which were to remove bone fragments and to drain abscesses which were embedded in the wounds. Because of the probing into the wounds by the doctors who failed to use sterilized instruments, the result was blood poisoning and the cause of the President's death.

After Garfield's request to be transferred by train to Elberon, New Jersey, he contracted bronchopneumonia there and two days later, he passed away.

A quote Garfield made in 1871, kindly sums up his stature for living: "I would rather believe something and suffer for it, than to slide along into success without opinions."

Again, a noble figure was slain for really no apparent reason except for vengeance of a warp-minded man who thought he was doing a service for his country by having Chester A. Arthur become President of the United States.

JESSE JAMES—1882

James Woodson James was born in Clay County, Missouri, on September 5th, 1847. His father, Robert S. James was of Welsh ancestry. His occupation was a commercial hemp farmer. In Kentucky he served the people as a Baptist minister. In Liberty, Missouri, he assisted in the foundation of William Jewell College.

After he got married, Robert moved back to Missouri. While there, he became very prosperous and accumulated more than one hundred acres of farmland. He, also, acquired six slaves when he moved there.

When Jesse was only three years of age, Robert died in California during the Gold Rush days while he administered to the gold diggers.

Jesse's mother was Zerelda Cole James who married twice after her husband's death. She first married a gentleman by the name of Benjamin Simms and later, to Dr. Reuben Samuel. Reuben and Zerelda had four children. The family became involved in tobacco cultivation in Missouri and acquired several slaves to work the fields.

The slave issue became an important focus in political events which finally ignited in a ghastly holocaust—the American Civil War.

The spark which started all this turmoil was the passage of the Kansas-Nebraska Act of 1854. The question was—would slavery be extended into Kansas.

There was a deluge of migrated Missourians into Kansas hoping to influence the voting there. The result of this political activity between the pro—and anti-slavery militias was bloodshed and violence.

Missouri, because of its entanglement in this crisis, was torn apart politically.

In 1861, guerrilla warfare split the state apart. A series of battles and campaigns were waged between the "bushwhackers" (secessionists) and the "jayhawkers" (Union local militia).

The atrocities were abundant as both sides engaged in the murder of civilians. Guerrillas went on a rampage and killed Union civilians, executed their prisoners, and even went to the extreme by scalping the dead.

Union forces retaliated, after hearing about the guerrilla atrocities, and enforced martial law. They arrested civilians who were guilty of killings; executed those who were found guilty; and Confederate sympathizers were banished from the state of Missouri.

The James' clan believed in the secessionist movement of the South and Frank James, brother of Jesse, joined Drew Lobbs' local company and fought at the battle of Wilson's Creek during the Civil War. He was later identified, in 1863, as a soldier of a squad of guerrillas that participated in war activities in Clay County.

In 1863, Union forces raided the James-Samuel farm while looking for Frank and his guerrilla buddies.

It was at this time, after eluding capture by a Union militia, that Frank decided to join William C. Quantrill's guerrilla organization.

Some people believe that he took part in the massacre of 200 boys and men in the abolitionist town of Lawrence, Kansas.

In 1863-1864, Frank went to Texas because Quantrill was going there. Then, he joined a squad led by Fletch Taylor. Franks' sixteen-year-old brother, Jesse, joined the group.

Later, Frank and Jesse joined Bloody Bill Anderson's bushwhacker group. It was with this group that Jesse and Frank participated in guerrilla activities. During the Centralia Massacre, the guerrillas killed some twenty-two unarmed Union troops. They even resorted to dismembering the dead soldiers and also scalped some of them.

Later, Major A. Johnson and Union troops pursued this guerrilla group but, were ambushed. When the troops tried to surrender, they were all killed. Jesse was given credit for fatally shooting the Major in the skirmish.

The Union military retaliated to these merciless killings by banishing Jesse's family from Clay County. They went to Nebraska instead of moving south as the decree indicated.

The James brothers separated after Bill Anderson was slain. Jesse went to Texas while Frank followed the Confederate leader, Quantrill, into

Kentucky. Archie Clement, who was one of Anderson's lieutenants, was in command of the squad in Texas and Jesse was under his command.

While Archie and Jesse tried to surrender after learning of a Confederate surrender near Lexington, Missouri, they ran into a patrol of Union Cavalry. At this juncture they had to decide what course they would follow in their operations. It was during this operation that Jesse was recovering from a second chest wound.

After the Civil War between the states, the Republican Party under President Abraham Lincoln took steps for reconstructing the South.

However, some of the terms were acerbic. Confederates were temporarily excluded from voting, becoming corporate officers, serving on juries, and from preaching from church pulpits. These were harsh infringements on their rights and led to volatile skirmishes between various factions.

When Jesse was recovering from his chest wound, he was nursed by his first cousin, Zerelda "Zee" Mimms. They finally got married after a long courtship which lasted some nine years.

Then, on February 13th, 1866, Archie Clement and his gang took part in the robbery of the Clay County Savings Association at Liberty, Missouri.

A tragedy occurred during this robbery. A bystander and a student of William Jewell College were killed during the gang's escape. There has never been any solid evidence that the James' brothers took part in this robbery at Clay County.

This was an era when Archie Clement and his notorious guerrillas kept up their works of looting and harassment of the Republican government. He was finally shot and killed by the state militia. Nevertheless, Clement's gang did not stop after his death as they continued their ruthless ways by robbing small local banks for the next two years.

On May 23rd, 1867, it has been recorded that they participated in the robbery of the Richmond, Missouri bank where they killed several men including the mayor.

In 1868, Jesse and Frank decided to join Cole Younger in robbing a bank located at Russellville, Kentucky. This union of lawlessness was recognized throughout the West as they robbed banks, trains, and stagecoaches. The gang robbed from Iowa all the way to Texas.

In 1869, Jesse James made the headlines in the newspapers as being the most famous of outlaws. The Missouri Governor, Thomas T. Crittenden set a huge reward of $10,000 for the capture of Jesse, dead or alive.

On July 21st, 1873, the Jesse-Younger gang began to rob trains—they derailed the Rock Island train in Adair, Iowa. This robbery garnered approximately three thousand dollars. In order to disguise themselves, they wore Ku Klux Klan masks. Jesse and his gang were more interested in robbing the express safes on the trains rather than holding up the passengers.

John Newman Edwards, who was the editor and founder of the Kansas City Times, had published letters from Jesse which had stated his innocence of the Gallatin robbery. These letters became very political over time as they denounced the Republicans in their Reconstruction documents.

These letters and the false image which he projected—"by robbing the rich and giving to the poor" (the money he robbed was only given to his gang) gave Jesse fame and notoriety.

Then, in 1874, the Adams Express Company hired the Pinkerton National Detective Agency to arrest the James-Younger gang. This agency wasn't too successful in Missouri as the gang was supported by Confederates who gave them shelter.

Joseph Whicher, an agent of the detective agency, was given the task of penetrating Zerelda Samuel's farm. He was later found dead. Then, on March 17th, 1874, two other agents, John Boyle and Louis Lull were killed by two members of the Younger gang in a roadside gunfight. Also, Edwin Daniels, a deputy sheriff, was killed in the gunfight.

Allan Pinkerton, the founder of the agency, was very bitter after his agents were slaughtered and took the case as a personal vendetta. Therefore, on January 25th, 1875 he raided the family farm.

His agents threw an explosive device into the house which killed James's half-brother Archie and blew off one of the arms of his mother Zerelda Samuel.

This raid created a heap of sympathy for Jesse James and many of his friends were outraged.

Later, the Missouri state legislature voted a limit on reward offers which the governor could make for outlaws. This vote actually gave protection to the James-Younger gang—especially to Frank and Jesse. This transaction was made possible because Confederates were again allowed to hold office and vote.

On September 7th, 1876, a raid on the First National Bank of Northfield, Minnesota by the James-Younger gang took place. After this robbery, a manhunt was taken which resulted in the capture of several members of Jesse's gang. Jesse and Frank escaped this capture.

In the melée, two of the bandits were killed because the citizens took part in the street fight. As they left the bank, one bandit shot the cashier, Heywood in the head.

After this gunfight, the James brothers escaped to Missouri and separated from the other members of the gang.

The militia finally caught up with the remaining Younger gang, killing one named Charlie Pitts and taking the rest of the gang prisoners.

Later, in 1876, the James' brothers took the names of Thomas Howard and B.J. Woodson when they arrived in Nashville, Tennessee. Here, Jesse gathered new members for his gang and began a series of crimes. At Glendale, Missouri, they held up a train. Later, he and his gang held up two more trains and robbed the federal paymaster of a canal project in Killen, Alabama. However, this gang didn't last long as some were captured and others fought each other. Jesse ended up killing one of the gang members and dismissing the others.

In 1881, the James' brothers decided to return to their home state of Missouri. Frank went to Virginia after Jesse rented a house in Saint Joseph, Missouri.

It was here that Jesse asked the Ford brothers, Charley and Robert, to move in with him and his family.

Bob, in the meantime, had been negotiating, secretly, with Thomas T. Crittenden, the Missouri governor, to bring in Jesse, as was previously stated, dead or alive.

On April 3rd, 1882, the Fords and James were getting ready for another robbery. As Jesse noticed a dusty picture on the wall, he stood on a chair to dust it off. While he was doing this, Bob snuck up behind him and shot Jesse in the back of the head.

Crittenden did grant the Fords pardons and the reward even though they were found guilty of murder.

Later, the Fords performed in a stage show in which they reenacted the shooting. On May 6th, 1884, Charley Ford, who had been suffering from tuberculosis and had an addiction to morphine, committed suicide in Richmond, Missouri. Charley's brother, Bob, owned a tent saloon in Creede, Colorado. Edward Capehart O'Kelley, on June 8th, 1892, killed Bob with a shotgun; the bullet penetrated his throat. He was sentenced to life in prison but, because of a medical impairment, his sentence was commuted and he was released on October 3rd, 1902.

Crittenden expected to receive fan fare for his involvement in the death of Jesse. However, the wheels of fortune turned against him. He didn't take into account Jesse's popularity. Crittenden had plans to elevate himself in politics. He hoped by the killing of Jesse he would win another term as governor, then, move into a Senate seat, and possibly become the United States President. However, everything backfired, and the citizens of Missouri refused to renominate him for governor. Because of this incident, his career went "down the drain".

After the end of the Reconstruction era, Jesse's crimes were placed emphatically in the content of America's historical writings which picture him as a celebrated Confederate bandit who supposedly robbed the rich and gave to the poor.

Some historians have relegated James' myth as a contribution to the upswing of former Confederates to higher positions in the politics of Missouri in the 1880's.

Dime novels have glorified the James Gang as hero bandits who resisted the pre-industrial giants of the era.

In the 1950's, James was regarded as a "psychologically troubled man rather than a social rebel".

WILLIAM MCKINLEY—1901

WHEN SCRUTINIZING THE PERSONALITY OF William McKinley, the 25th President of the United States, a man of integrity, friendliness, cool-headed, passive at times but cautious, well-liked among his colleagues and the public at large, all these qualities come to the fore.

The biographer, Charles S. Olcott sums this up very thoroughly when he stated: "His uniform courtesy and fairness commanded the admiration of Democrats as well as Republicans, etc . . ."

McKinley was of Scotch-Irish descent who took his name from his father, dropping the "junior" when his father died. His mother was Nancy Allison McKinley. He was born on January 29th, 1843, in Niles, Ohio. His wife was Ida Saxton who was born on June 8th, 1847, in Canton, Ohio.

McKinley came from a large family—three brothers and four sisters. He had two daughters, Ida and Katherine McKinley.

His early life came close to a tragedy when he nearly drowned in Mosquito Creek. He spent the remainder of his childhood in Poland, Ohio.

McKinley's education centered at an early age in the public schools of Niles, Ohio. In 1852, he enrolled at the Poland Seminary which was a Methodist institution. He was regarded as a very elegant speaker and was selected as the first president of the school's Everett Literary and Debating Society. When he reached 17 years of age, he entered Allegheny College at Meadville, Pennsylvania. Unfortunately, here he became ill and was forced to drop out. Because of a lack of finances due to the depression following the Panic of 1857, he was forced to forget about school and to seek a job. He held several jobs at this time of depression—one as a teacher at the Kerr District School in Poland and later as a clerk at the town post office. Later, he served in the Civil War with the Twenty-third

Ohio Volunteer Infantry and working his way "up the ladder" to the rank of second lieutenant under Colonel Rutherford B. Hayes.

During this conflagration, McKinley demonstrated his courage and determination by engaging in several battles. He first saw action at Carnifex Ferry, West Virginia in September of 1861. The following year, 1862, he was engaged in the battles of Clark's Hollow and Princeton, West Virginia, and also South Mountain.

However, he received great praise and laurels for his heroism when he delivered, under fire, rations to the troops serving on the front lines at Antietam in September of 1862. As was mentioned earlier, for this heroic act he was promoted to second lieutenant. Another incident in which he showed his bravery was when he carried orders to the front under fire in order to retrieve artillery. After this engagement, he was promoted to captain. He, also, served on the staffs of Generals Winfield S. Hancock and George Crook. Because of these heroic acts, he was promoted to brevet major.

Rutherford B. Hayes had nothing but praise for a young soldier who gave his all in a time of crisis.

Then, after the war, in 1867, he was admitted to the bar and set up his office in Canton, Ohio. It was at this time that he became affiliated with the Republican Party.

Gaining notoriety in this position, he became very famous with the populace and was elected as prosecutor of Stark County in 1869.

Then, in 1871, he was forced to resume his practice as a lawyer when he failed to be reelected as the prosecutor of the County.

Eventually, he entered politics and was elected U.S. Representative in 1876 on the Republican ticket, representing Ohio's Eighteenth District. At this position, he pleased westerners by voting for the Bland-Allison Act. This Act was enacted over President Hayes's veto. The Democratic Representative Richard Bland of Missouri and Republican Senator William B. Allison of Iowa sponsored this measure. The bill was intended to inflate the currency which would benefit debtors, farmers and silver miners. It stated that the federal government would purchase $2-$4 million worth of silver each month for coinage.

However, the legislation for this bill was overridden by the Sherman Silver Purchase Act of 1890. By this Act, the United States Treasury was required to purchase at market price 4.5 million ounces of silver per month. Notes redeemable in silver or gold would purchase the silver.

This transaction had a very serious ripple effect on the federal reserves by depleting them to a significant degree as the holders of these notes promptly redeemed them for gold.

At this juncture, McKinley's reputation blossomed in the national arena of the House of Representatives as he became known as the champion of protectionism. He was in favor of a high tariff as a protective measure for national self-defense against the goods which were coming from foreign countries.

He became governor of Ohio from 1892-1896, defeating the Democrat, James E. Campbell in October of 1891. Later, he defeated Lawrence T. Neal for the same position.

As governor, he was forced to call out the National Guard to stifle a labor relations outburst in Akron, Cleveland and other disturbed places in the state. He became very active at this time in politics—secured safety measures in transportation, placed an excise tax on corporations, and took on the employers of big business by restricting their practice of anti-unionism.

Then, in the presidential election of 1896, McKinley was on the top of the list of the Republican Party. The final push that elevated him to the top was the Cleveland multimillionaire, Mark Hanna.

The election introduced a great speaker of the Democratic Party whose "Cross of Gold" speech has gone down in history—his name was William Jennings Bryan of Nebraska. He stubbornly insisted that the silver plank be posted on all the campaign issues. Without it, he said, he would refuse the nomination. As a result, the silver plank was accepted.

In 1897, McKinley, in his first annual message to Congress, notified Spain that it must change its policies toward Cuba.

Then, in 1898, the United States battleship Maine was blown up and sank in the Havana Harbor in Cuba killing 266 Americans. Spain was blamed for the incident but later investigations showed that it was a boiler on the ship that caused the explosion.

However, because of all the adverse publicity in the 'yellow' pages of the William R. Hearst New York Journal and his rival, Joseph Pulitzer who competed with him for top headlines, both contributed to the war cry which rang out: "Remember the Maine! The Hell with Spain!"

President McKinley had hoped to avert the Cuban conflict without involving the intervention of the United States military. However, that would not be the case.

Spain severed relations with the United States after McKinley got the OK from Congress authorizing him to intervene in Cuba in order to force the Spanish withdrawal. McKinley immediately ordered a blockade of Cuban ports. Seeing that this move was a clear act of aggression, Spain declared war on the United States on April 23rd, 1898. The United States followed suit and declared war on Spain on April 25th, 1898. The United States were the victors and gained the territories of Cuba, Guam, Puerto Rico, and the Philippine Islands. The United States eventually paid Spain $20 million for the Philippines for their loss. Negotiations for the peace treaty took place in Paris. At this time, Congress passed a joint resolution which was called the Teller Amendment which disclaimed any intention of the United States taking over Cuba's sovereignty or control over the jurisdiction of the island, except for peaceful means.

Nevertheless, the United States government took official control of Cuba in 1899 and formed a military government until local government was formed in 1902 and became a U.S. protectorate until 1934.

Because the U.S. annexed the Philippine Islands in 1899, Emilio Aquinaldo, a Filipino nationalist gathered forces and attacked the U.S. forces in Manila which commenced the Philippine-American War. The U.S. finally, after two years of warfare, crushed the rebellion.

Eventually, both Cuba and the Philippines secured their independence—the Philippines on July 4th, 1946 and Cuba, 1901.

McKinley retained the Philippines as a naval station and as an American protectorate. These ideas were already discussed when Theodore Roosevelt and Alfred Thayer Mahan laid out plans for the United States to become a world power and to obtain the islands in the Pacific as overseas coaling stations.

Hawaii joined the wagon of annexed islands in 1893 when Queen Liliuokalani gave up her throne to make way for a republic. It was the action of pro-American businessmen who "turned the tables" on the Queen and forced her to step down. McKinley made the rash comment when he stated: "It is manifest destiny. We need Hawaii just as much . . . as we did California."

The United States finally took its place among the world powers and was committed to an Open Door policy for trade with the Chinese. The leading exponent of this policy of the United States was John Hay, Secretary of State. He was in favor of a United States overseas empire and also wanted to cooperate with Great Britain in achieving his Open Door Policy. In 1899 he sent notes to the various powers who had a hold on China's assets. He requested that these powers keep the ports of China open to vessels from all nations on equal terms. He, also, wanted all the invested nations with China to levy equal tariffs on imports and charge equal railroad rates where they had business contacts with other countries.

The result of this meddling in the internal affairs of China resulted in a rebellion of Chinese patriots who called themselves "Fists of Universal Harmony." The rebellion got the name Boxer Rebellion because of this organization. By the time it was subdued, they had slain over 200 missionaries including several Catholic bishops in the process. Even women and children weren't exempt from this slaughter.

The United States sent a task force of 2,500 troops and other countries joined to quell this uprising.

The United States government paid the Chinese government around 25 million dollars to help pay off its indemnity for its backing of the Boxer Rebellion.

As a good will gesture by the United States, it returned 11 million dollars to the Chinese government in 1907. This money was used to educate the Chinese in the universities throughout the United States.

McKinley was reelected in 1900 and his vice-president was Theodore Roosevelt who had been the governor of New York.

"The full dinner pail" became the Republican slogan in the election and they won by a large majority of votes.

In September of 1901, six months after his inauguration, all "hell broke loose." In Buffalo, New York, he was asked to speak about commercial exchange among nations at the Pan American Exposition. Here, he was greeting guests at the Temple of Music Hall. A young man named Leon Czolgosz, an anarchist, approached McKinley with a handkerchief on his left hand which looked like a bandage.

As McKinley reached out to grasp Leon's hand, he was shot in the stomach with a .32 caliber Iver Johnson revolver. McKinley didn't die suddenly but lived for more than a week. He finally succumbed to that fatal bullet in the stomach. The last words which he uttered were: "It is God's way. His will be done, not ours. We are all going, we are all going, oh dear." McKinley was only fifty-eight years old.

Again, a great man who died before his time—a man of kindness, gentleness, and a love for his country.

FRANZ FERDINAND—1914

WHO WOULD HAVE THOUGHT THAT shots from a Serbian youth, age 19, would have ignited WWI on June 28th, 1914, sometimes called The Great War. The first bullet had struck the Archduke of Austria-Hungary in the neck which severed a jugular vein and the second bullet struck his wife, Sophie Chotek, the Duchess of Hohenburg, in the stomach.

Immediately, Austria-Hungary discussed plans on how to punish the Serbs for the killing of Franz Ferdinand.

Not wanting to give the world the impression that Austria-Hungary was an aggressor, she delivered a ten point ultimatum to Serbia, giving her 48 hours in which to comply. One principle of this ultimatum stated that a judicial inquiry be held whereby representatives of Austria-Hungary would be involved.

Rejecting this offer, as it violated the Serbian Constitution and its criminal code, Serbia, in order to avoid war, suggested the issue be referred to the International Court at The Hague in the Netherlands.

Austria rejected this suggestion and Emperor Franz Joseph of Vienna, Austria, mobilized an army in preparation for war. When news of this mobilization reached Russia, they too, began to mobilize as she regarded herself as the protector of the Balkan Slavs.

The Germans told the Russians to immobilize their forces and also asked France to remain neutral in case of a war breaking out between Russia and Germany.

However, France and Russia were not intimidated by these demands and resulted in a declaration of war between Germany and Russia.

Before long, Britain took sides with Russia and France which formed an alliance called the Triple Entente. These countries were opposed by the Triple Alliance of Germany, Austria-Hungary, and Italy. Later, Turkey joined the Alliance while the United States took sides with Russia.

When WWI broke out, many thought the war would last only a few weeks. No one realized that new technologies of arms, such as, tanks, machine guns, submarine, large size canons, airplanes, flame throwers and poison gas used by the Germans would prolong the war. The outcome was a stalemate as armies on both sides got bogged down in muddy trenches. The casualties on both sides were tremendous.

On the first day in the battle of the Somme, the British took a "pounding" and lost 19,000 dead and about 60,000 casualties.

Several battles, in which the Entente was victorious, were at Verdun and at Marne. However, at Gallipoli, in Turkey, the Anzacs, composed of Australian and New Zealand recruits, took a heavy beating—many died from heat exhaustion.

The same may be said of the number of casualties which took place on the Western Front—due to the harsh conditions in the trenches, many men contacted tuberculosis and died.

It has been estimated that the total number of dead was 8.5 million and 20 million wounded. The direct cost of the war seems incalculable, 200 billion dollars.

What a price to be paid in men and property. If these sums were required to be doled out for peace, social justice, and economic achievements instead of war, what a savings in human life and suffering would have been achieved.

Stated previously, the spark that ignited this conflagration was the assassination of Franz Ferdinand and his wife, Sophie, on June 28th, 1914.

On June 28th, the royal couple was greeted by the governor of the province of Bosnia-Herzegovina, General Oskar Potiorek. After they left the train and were greeted by the General, they entered a limousine which took them to a reception at the Town Hall.

The procession drove along Appel Quay. However, along the way, were Bosnia's young men who belonged to a secret society called the Black Hand who viewed Austria as a tyrannical country. They felt that Franz and his uncle, Emperor Franz Joseph I, were cruel oppressors who dominated their lives under the Hapsburg regime. They resented the fact that they weren't able to unite with the neighboring state of Serbia which was connected to Bosnia at one time.

As they rode along this route, six of the Black Hand members were stationed in the crowd. As the procession drove slowly across the Cumurija Bridge, a young man, by the name of Nedeljko Cabrinovic, emerged from the crowd, took a bomb from his belt, and heaved it at the car carrying the Archduke.

Fortunately, the bomb landed on the roof of the car and bounced off into the street. The bomb went off under a car which was following the Duke's car. Two officers in the car were bleeding profusely—one from a head wound and other spectators were bleeding from flying fragments of the bomb.

When Franz reached the Town Hall, he visited one of his injured aides who had been taken to a nearby military hospital.

After this incident, the Archduke and his wife headed back along the Appel Quay. As they proceeded, General Potiorek told the driver that he was going the wrong way. The driver, then, stopped the car and proceeded to back up. Little did they know that a young man, age 19, emerged from the crowd carrying a Russian Browning pistol and fired two shots at the Archduke and his wife. His name was Gavrilo Princip, a national fanatic.

As was stated earlier, one bullet struck the Archduke in the neck and the other pierced Sophie's stomach.

The car was then driven to the governor's residence but there was nothing the doctors could do to save their lives.

They were later taken to the railway station under a military escort and escorted to their home in Vienna.

Gavrilo was the "principal defendant at the trial of the five members of the Black Hand for murder and high treason." Because of their ages, both Cabrinovic and Princip were not given the death sentence, but instead, were sentenced to 20 years of hard labor. Princip, later, died of tuberculosis in 1918 in a hospital. He was only 23 years of age at the time.

So, the royal family's visit ended in a horrible tragedy of two outstanding people whose only mistake was going to a country, Bosnia, where the Archduke of Austria-Hungry was asked to give an address of appeasement between the two warring factions.

This touchy situation had troubled the two nations for quite some time. The problem was over territory which both countries claimed after the Balkan wars of 1912. Serbia had won its freedom and independence from the Ottoman Turkish Empire and had doubled its size by its victories during the Balkan wars. These victories caused a feeling of nationalism which pervaded the entire country and provoked an upsurge of hostility against the Austro-Hungarian Empire who had oppressed the southern Slavs of Bosnia-Herzegovina.

As a result of all this hostility, the Archduke and his wife were assassinated. This triggered the fatalistic and bloody battles of WWI.

GRIGORI YEFIMOVICH RASPUTIN—1916

AFTER READING ABOUT THE LIFE of Nicholas II, the Czar of Russia, his assassination and his family, this author came across another interesting character who also entered the realm of assassinations. This monk lived a life of intrigue and fascination which shook the world at that time, especially, in the political arena of Russian politics.

To summarize the life of Rasputin, it is imperative to break down the events of his life in several segments which gives a clear picture of what he did to jeopardize the government of Russia and the Russian people.

To justify this summation, it was necessary to arrange these events in an orderly manner, beginning with his early life and ending with his horrible assassination in 1916.

Rasputin was born on January 22nd, 1869 in Pokrovskoye, Siberia. He was often referred to as the "Mad Monk" and sometimes the "Black Monk." Others considered him a "strannik" (religious pilgrim) and at times he was called a starets (holy man), a title usually given to monk-confessors. He was also believed to be a faith healer and a psychic. Some contemporary scholars saw him as a healer, mystic, and even a prophet. Others claimed that he was a religious quack.

However, there have been various accounts of his life which have been seen as dubious and unfounded—sometimes hearsay.

Rasputin's early life was filled with tragedy which summarily affected his personality—his sister, Maria, who had epilepsy, drowned in a river and his brother, Dmitri, had fallen into a pond and later died of pneumonia.

Several myths grew up about his childhood. One such myth stated that he had supernatural powers. For example, when his father Efim Rasputin had one of his horses stolen, the young Rasputin identified the man who had stolen the animal.

Rasputin was put in a monastery when he was about eighteen years of age and had to spend three months there.

It has also been claimed that Rasputin was a member of the Khlysts, a flagellant religious group which hurt his reputation.

Being charged as a member by Alexander Guchkov, the Tsar ordered an investigation of the charges and found that these were empty and unfounded and did not require removal of Rasputin from his influential position. Instead, he fired his minister of the interior for not controlling this false propaganda in the press.

When Rasputin left the monastery, he came across a holy man named Makariy who greatly influenced him and became his model for life.

Later on, Rasputin got married to Praskovia Dubrovina in 1889 with whom he had three children—Maria, Dmitri, and Varvara.

Then, in 1901, he "got the itch" for traveling and embarked on a journey to Jerusalem and Greece. He, finally, arrived in St. Petersburg in 1903 where, as a holy man (starets), he developed a reputation for healing and having prophetic powers.

While wandering in Siberia, he heard of Alexis's illness, the son of the Czarina Alexandra, wife of czar, Nicholas II, emperor of Russia.

Czarina became emotionally frustrated when she couldn't get help from the doctors. It was at this juncture that she turned for help from her good friend Anna Vyrubova, who, in turn, sought the help of Rasputin in 1905. Rasputin was called upon, time after time, to stop the bleeding internally as well as externally, from hemophilia which her son Alexis had inherited from his mother. How Rasputin achieved this stoppage is not known. Some people said that he used hypnosis. Others have even suggested that he used leeches to treat the ailing boy

Unknowingly, the child subsequently got better and this invoked a great deal of confidence in the monk.

Nicholas and his wife, Alexandra, had great faith in Rasputin and considered him to be a man of God. Alexandra came to the conclusion that God was talking to her through the "prophet," Rasputin. Rasputin eventually became a great influence, both personally and politically, on the Czar and Czarina.

Nevertheless, the nobility of St. Petersburg did not take a liking to Rasputin because he did not come from royalty and was regarded as evil and immoral.

The Orthodox Church, on several occasions, accused him of various immoral activities. These reports seem to be accurate for, being a court official, he was under constant surveillance by the police spies who gave credible evidence to the newspapers, and also, to the Tsar himself.

Rasputin had a very different outlook on spirituality. He spoke of salvation as "depending less on the clergy and the church than on seeking the spirit of God within."

He also claimed that repentance and sin were necessary for salvation and were dependent on each other. In order to achieve both salvation and repentance, he had the strange idea that it was necessary to have sex and alcohol and yield to temptation.

He thought war was immoral and that it would eventually lead to a political upheaval and a curse to society.

Therefore, he condemned WWI and the effect it had on the Russian people—famine, poverty, loss of homes, and repression.

As a result, he was regarded as being very unpatriotic and disloyal to the cause. In order to rectify this concept, Rasputin expressed an interest in going to the front to prove his patriotism and to allay any doubts the Russian people may have had of him. This provoked the animosity of Nicholas and he said that he would have him "hanged" if he showed up at the front.

In response to this accusation, Rasputin responded to the Tsar that he had a revelation that the Russian armies would be defeated unless the Tsar went to the front and personally took command.

While the emperor was away, Rasputin's influence increased tremendously with Czarina, Alexandra. She filled government positions on his advise and he, in turn, picked some of his close friends to occupy important positions in the government. The result of all this adverse propaganda was a weakening of government, jealously and bitterness among the Russian elite and, talk of getting rid of this incorrigible mad man.

Vladimir Purishkevich spoke to the Duma, the legislative body, on November 19th, 1916, in which he condemned Rasputin for the failing economy, and also, the Empress, Alexandra, a German, whom he implied was an alien of Russia.

Felix Yusupov, who heard the speech, immediately contacted Purishkivich and agreed to participate in the murder of Rasputin.

Nobles and legislators of the Duma clamored for the removal of Rasputin from court. Because of this adverse publicity, Nicholas loss favor and popularity with the Russian people and was later asked to abdicate by the nobility.

When revolution broke out in February 1917, Nicholas left his headquarters on the Russian front to return to Petrograd.

However, his train stopped at Pskov. It was here that he heard that all of his ministers had resigned and he in turn followed suit and did likewise.

The plot to do away with Rasputin was instigated at Petrograd (St. Petersburg) at the Moika Palace where Prince Felix Yussupov lived. He and four others decided on the kill on December 30ᵗʰ, 1916, during the post-Christmas celebrations.

At the palace, Rasputin was received with royalty and imbibed with alcohol and refreshments. After several glasses of wine, the prince escorted Rasputin down the stairway to a plush basement which was on display with fine artworks and crystal mirrors.

It was here that Rasputin was given several cakes which he took most cordially. These cakes were filled with cyanide which, evidently, proved ineffective in killing Rasputin.

Yusupov ran upstairs to talk to the other conspirators and to obtain a Browning revolver. When he came down to the basement, he shot Rasputin in the back.

Yusupov had gone outside and came indoors to procure a coat. Here, he went to check on Rasputin's condition and found that he was still alive. As the prince bent down, Rasputin lunged at him and attempted to strangle him. The other conspirators came down the stairway and began to fire shots at Rasputin. Rasputin was shot three more times in the back.

However, as they neared his body, they discovered that he was still alive and tried to get up. They finally invoked his coup-de-grace by clubbing him to death. They proceeded to wrap his body in a sheet and then threw him in the Neva River.

Finally, came the demise of an intriguing and immoral man bent on getting his way at all costs. An obstinate and callous individual met his death by royal conspirators who felt it necessary to eliminate him because the government was in a state of turmoil and on the verge of collapsing.

Lenin, a Bolshevik, who had signed a peace treaty with the Germans in March of 1918, realizing this state of urgency, took advantage of the situation and became the first premier of post Imperial Russia. He had the Czar, Nicholas II and his family executed when he took over the Russian government in 1918.

NICHOLAS II—1918

THERE WERE SEVERAL EVENTS WHICH led to the overthrow of the Romanov dynasty and the assassination of Nicholas II and his family. These events, in the order of succession, which sparked the flames and which led to the Russian Resolution of 1917 were: the bloody massacre which occurred on Sunday, January 22nd, 1905, the poverty, famine, and grievances which the Russian people were enduring at that time, the corrupt and inefficient government in which Rasputin played a major part when the Czar was away at the front in WWI directing operations. At this time, Nicholas positioned his friends in government and directed his own policies which had an adverse effect on the government and eventually brought on the Bolshevik Revolution. The Russian troops fighting the Germans in WWI were ill-equipped with fighting weapons to win a war of this magnitude; the final collapse of the Russian government and hierarchy came when Vladimir Lenin came to power and headed the Bolshevik Socialist Democratic Labor Party (later renamed the Russian Communist Party) which ushered in the Soviet age.

In 1905, a disgruntled and poverty stricken Russian populace, in the dead of winter, surged on the Czar's Winter Palace located at St. Petersburg. They were led by a bearded priest named Father Georgei Gapon. Father Gapon had worked as a missionary in the poor slums of St. Petersburg, and also, was a friend at the court of Nicholas II.

In 1904, he authorized the formation of Russian Factory Workers who were discontented with the things which were happening, especially, at the Putilov Ironworks in St. Petersburg. Their demands were of the usual type, better working conditions, higher wages, and an eight-hour day.

Soon thereafter, the city was on the verge of a general strike. Lenin, who was exiled in Switzerland at the time, commented that Russia was on the verge of a political strike.

It was during this crucial period that Father Gapon drew up an appeal to be presented to the Tsar at the Winter Palace.

The petition asked for a society of equality and freedom. Also, they wanted to vote for an assembly in secret without any outside interference or coercion.

As the workers approached the Palace Square, they were refused permission to enter. This aroused a great deal of emotion and outburst in the crowd. The Cossack guards on duty shot into the crowd killing about one hundred and fifty people—women, children and men. Statics have shown some five hundred people lost their lives.

Father Gapon had miscalculated because he thought that the guards and troops guarding the Narva gate would join the protesters.

Gapon narrowly escaped death and he was given shelter by the revolutionary novelist, Maxim Gorky. Later, he fled to Geneva where he became friends with Lenin. He eventually returned to Russia and, in 1906, he was accused of being a government spy. He was hanged in a cottage on the Finnish border located near St. Petersburg.

Even though the outbreak of 1905 was unsuccessful in changing any reforms in government, it did awake the feelings of the Russian people toward their government and, after a reign of twelve years, Nicholas was the last tsar to rule Russia.

Another grievance, which had a major effect on the people, was the corruptible and disorganized government of Gregory Rasputin, a quasi-holy man, who became an advisor to Czar Nicholas II and his wife Alexandra. It is interesting to note that he achieved this recognition by treating their son, Alexis, who was a hemophiliac.

The Duma, the legislative assembly, realized the harmful effects that Rasputin was having on the government. At one time, they tried to exile him, but failed.

As the government became weaker so did Nicholas II's reputation and he became distrusted by the Russian populace.

A grave and significant grievance was Nicholas II's indifference to the war effort of 1917.

The armies were so short of weapons that some soldiers were sent into the foray without guns and were told to pick up those of the soldiers who had been killed.

The Germans were taking a huge toll of Russian troops—more than five million were killed or wounded.

This disaster, on the front lines, set off bread riots in Petrograd on March 8th, 1917. This incident ignited a strike of workers whereby sailors and soldiers joined the ranks. These workers formed a council that demanded Nicholas' abdication. Then, on March 15th, the Duma (legislative body) suggested to Nicholas, that for the good of the country, he relinquish his throne.

A provisional government was formed which promised all sorts of reforms. This government proved to be ineffective and disorganized and was soon replaced in July by a second government under the inspiring Leader Alexsandr Kerensky.

He tried but failed to continue the fight against Germany. Then, on November 7th, his regime was overthrown by the Bolshevik Revolution.

In April 1917, the Germans in order to weaken the Russian government, made plans to send Lenin there from his exile in Switzerland where he spent time writing about Marxism and revolutionary tactics. With the help of Leon Trotsky who had been exiled in New York and had returned to Russia, he overthrew the Kerensky government and replaced it with the Bolshevik regime. Here, they began to refer themselves as Communists.

Lenin knew what the Russian people wanted and his slogan was of Peace, Land, Bread and was used to brighten the hopes of a grieving and poverty-stricken people.

The Bolsheviks and Lenin were thoroughly against the war. His interest was ingrained with the Communist party and he did all he could to advance it.

Therefore, in March 1918, Russia signed a peace treaty at Brest-Litovsk with the Central Powers (Germany, Austria-Hungary and Turkey). Russia gave up territories in the south and west which included the Ukraine wheat lands. These territories which were forwarded to Germany were Finland, Moldavia, Belarus, Poland and included the Baltic States of Lithuania, Latvia, and Estonia.

The Bolsheviks had the Romanov family of Nicholas II arrested and placed in a cellar in Ekaterinburg in the Ural mountains in July of 1918. Here, they were slain and buried.

There has been a good deal of controversy about the skeletal bones concerning the actuality of the Nicholas family. These bones were found in a pit in eastern Russia in 1991. The bone samples were sent to Britain for analysis and DNA tests. They were compared with the blood of the Duke of Edinburgh, a relative of Alexandra, and two living descendants of the Tsar.

The results were incredible. They proved with a 99 per cent degree of certainty that those skeletons found were those of the Nicholas' family.

So, a great regime finally came to an end. In its place, a brutal and merciless government under Joseph Stalin emerged. Before he died in March, 1953, he left in his wake the death of thousands of innocent people who disagreed with his policies.

DUTCH SCHULTZ—1935

DUTCH SCHULTZ, A NOTORIOUS GANGSTER, (real name Arthur Flegenheimer) was born in the Bronx, New York, in 1902. He was of Jewish descent and made his fortune in illegal alcohol, bootlegging, and the numbers racket which he controlled in Harlem, New York.

At the time, in the twenties and thirties, the underworld was at its peak in organized crime. Dutch was in competition with another cold-hearted gangster, Charles "Lucky" Luciano, who was the head of a crime syndicate in New York.

In 1935, Thomas E. Dewey of New York had succeeded in convicting several major criminals and had them put in jail. Dewey had great ambitions and had eventually used his campaign against organized crime as a leap toward the governorship of New York. Later, he campaigned for the presidency of the United States but failed in this attempt. This attempt for the two positions from a neophyte prosecutor would have been a tremendous move in the political arena.

Dewey's reputation increased tremendously when he had the notorious Waxey Gordon, Gurrah Shapiro, Louis Lepke, and most of all, the ring leader, "Lucky" Luciano convicted of crimes. Dewey became known as the "racket buster."

Because Dewey was after Schultz, who was the chief operator in New York's Harlem rackets, Schultz feared he was next on Dewey's list to be taken into custody. Schultz had a great reputation as one of the leading gangsters for, in 1931, he was a founding member of the National Crime Syndicate.

Schultz appeared before the National Syndicate Board with a plan to assassinate Dewey because the latter was investigating Schultz's operations and getting too much information about his adverse activities.

However, in 1931, the syndicate, not wanting any adverse publicity that would be detrimental to their operations, forbade the killing of district attorneys, police, or newspaper reporters. Therefore, the board turned down Schultz's plan in which Luciano and gangster Meyer Lansky took an active part in the negation.

Nevertheless, Schultz decided to carry out his plan despite the failure of the board to approve it.

In 1935, the board realized that Schultz was sincere in committing the act and that he was not faking his intent and just "letting out steam".

Schultz had Dewey's Fifth Avenue apartment staked out everyday. Dewey had a habit of making a phone call from a payphone at a drug store each morning to his office. The reason for this unusual activity was because he felt that his home phone might be tapped.

Knowing Dewey's routine each morning, Schultz went ahead with his plot to assassinate him. Therefore, Schultz placed one of his men inside the store equipped with a silencer gun.

Schultz had hired a killer named Albert Anastasia who was to do the killing not knowing that he was a friend of Luciano to whom he gave the information about the plot.

Luciano and his henchmen immediately took action to prevent the assassination.

Then, on October 23rd, 1935, at the Palace Chop House and Tavern in Newark, New Jersey which was Schultz's gang's favorite hangout, he and three of his men, Abe Landau, Abbadabba Berman, and Lulu Rosenkrantz met.

While Schultz went to the bathroom to urinate, two hit men came into the Tavern. One of the hit men came into the men's room, not knowing that it was Schultz in there, and shot him point blank. Then, he entered the room where three of Schultz's men were seated and "blazed away" killing all three.

After the killing, the two gunmen left the tavern. One of them removed a great amount of money from Schultz's pockets as he laid on the bathroom floor in a heap of blood.

Schultz was rushed to a hospital and lived for two days before he succumbed. One of the killers was Charles "the bug" Workman who was eventually convicted of the crime and served twenty-three years in prison.

In 1940, Dewey learned of the plot against him by Murder Inc. prosecutor, Burton Turkus.

There have been several reasons given for Schultz's assassination. One was the desire of syndicate leaders to take over Schultz's rackets.

Eventually, it did actually happen as other mobs took over his racket empire. The other reason given and, the main motivation, was to save Dewey's life in order to avoid bias attention to the syndicate if the prosecutor were killed.

Schultz left millions of dollars when he died which have never been accounted for.

Finally, a notorious and heartless gangster "bit the dust" and, several years later, Luciano and his mobsters were convicted of crimes against society.

LEON TROTSKY, RUSSIAN REVOLUTIONARY LEADER—1940

Leon Trotsky was born Lev Davidovich Bronstein on November 7th, 1879, in Yanovka Kherson Province of the Russian Empire. His father was David Leontyevich Bronstein who was a farmer of means, and Anna Bronstein, his mother. Trotsky's younger sister was Olga who married a prominent Bolshevik by the name of Lev Kamenev.

Trotsky received a fairly decent education. His father took an interest in his educational development by sending him off to Odessa where he enrolled in a German historical school. While there, he gained a great deal of insight in international affairs. One writer, Raymond Molinier, has claimed that he spoke French very fluently.

Trotsky became involved in politics right after his schooling. In 1896, when he moved to Nikolayev (now Mykolaiv), he became involved in political activities. Early in his career, he was exposed to Marxism but rejected it. However, when he was imprisoned and exiled, he accepted it. Then, in 1897, he was instrumental in organizing the South Russian Workers' Union in Nikolayev. By writing and distributing leaflets and pamphlets among revolutionary students and industrial workers, his intent was to indoctrinate them into the political arena of socialism. The Union grew in numbers for, in January, 1898, it could only tally 200 members. However, because of their adverse activities, they were arrested and, Trotsky, a member also, was to spend the next two years in prison awaiting his trial.

It was during his imprisonment that the first Congress of the new Russian Social Democratic Labor Party held its meeting. Trotsky, then, joined the party.

While he was in prison, two bizarre things happened. First, he got married to a Marxist, Aleksandra Sokolovskaya. Second, he became interested in philosophy which he studied most ardently.

Then, in 1900, he was again sentenced to prison and spent four years in exile in Ust-Kut and Verkholensk, Siberia, where his two daughters were born, Nina Nevelson and Zinaida Volkova.

In 1900, a London newspaper, Iskra, was founded which believed that an efficient organizational revolutionary party was necessary to cope with the differences expressed by the party members. Trotsky was impressed with their view and joined the group who believed in the Iskra philosophy.

While in London he joined the Iskra newspaper group, comprised of six editors, among whom were Lenin, Martov, and George Plekhanov. In a short while, Trotsky gained recognition as one of the leading authors of the newspaper and wrote under the pen name Pero, (in Russian language, "pen" or "feather").

The six editors of Iskra were split in their preference for party objectives. The "old guard" was led by Plekhanov while the "new guard" was led by Lenin and Martov.

Lenin tried to lure Trotsky in joining the New Guard in March, 1903, by writing an article which emphasized all the good qualities which Trotsky possessed and why he would become an elegant asset to the board.

However, Trotsky did not become a full member of the board due to Plekhanov's opposition.

It was during this period of bickering between the two parties that Trotsky met Natalia Sedova and married her in 1903. They had two children—Lev Sedov and Sergei Sedov.

Trotsky's first wife, Aleksandra Sokolovskaya, disappeared in 1935 during the Great Purges. He and she had, up to that time, a friendly relationship.

After the 2nd Congress met in London in 1903, the pro-Iskra delegates split into two groups. Martov was a close friend of Lenin and he and his supporters, the Mensheviks, desired a large and undisciplined party; whereas, Lenin, on the other hand, with his followers the Bolsheviks, desired a smaller but well-organized party.

An uncanny result emerged from this controversy—Plekhanov took sides with Lenin and his Bolsheviks while, Trotsky, to the surprise of others, joined the Iskra editors, and supported Martov and the Mensheviks. These arrangements didn't last long, however, as both parties changed sides in 1903 and 1904.

Trotsky, in 1904 and 1917, tried very fervently, to reconcile the parties' differences which resulted in many disputes and fighting with Lenin's associates. Trotsky and Lenin finally became friends when Trotsky acknowledged his wrong-doing when referring to the party's policy.

In the years between 1904 and 1907, Trotsky and Alexander Parvus worked together when Trotsky began working on his theory of "permanent revolution".

After a secret police agent had betrayed the local Menshevik committee, a radical group, which Trotsky supported most vociferously, he was forced to flee to Finland where he ardently worked on his theory of permanent revolution.

After a brief sojourn in Finland, he returned to Russia's capital, St. Petersburg.

Here, he and Parvus founded a newspaper called <u>Nachalo</u> ("The Beginning") with the assistance of the Mensheviks which turned out to be a major success.

By the time that Trotsky arrived in St. Petersburg, an organization called the first Soviet Council of Workers was functioning. Trotsky, impressed with their agenda, joined the group and was elected as vice-chairman. Then, on the 26th of November, the head of the organization, Khrustalev-Nosar, was arrested, and Trotsky became its chairman. The arrests continued for, on December 3rd, the Soviet deputies were arrested by governmental troops.

Trotsky, with other Soviet members, were tried on charges of giving their approval and support to the rebels.

Trotsky was tried and deported after his trial and his reputation was enhanced because he became an effective public speaker during his trial. While on route to Siberia in January, 1907, Trotsky managed to escape and headed for London once again. There, he attended the 5th Congress of the Russian Social Democratic Labor Party.

After this meeting, he went to Vienna, Austria, where he took part in the Austrian Social Democratic Party activities, and also, with the German Social Democratic Party. He was engaged in these activities for a period of seven years.

While he was in Vienna, he came into contact with Adolph Joffee who became his personal friend for twenty years.

During this period, Trotsky became interested in psychoanalysis which Joffee introduced him to. Then, in 1908, he and Joffee commenced writing a paper which was called the <u>Pravda</u> ("Truth"), which dealt with Russian workers, and also, was a bi-weekly Russian language paper. With the assistance of their co-workers, Kopp and Shobelev, they were able to smuggle this paper into Russia.

Trotsky's paper Pravda, became so popular that it became a party-financed operative at a meeting held in Paris in January, 1910. Eventually, this paper folded in April of 1912 after operating for another two years.

Trotsky and the Mensheviks had several disagreements with Lenin besides the unification issue between the Bolsheviks and the Mensheviks. One such disagreement dealt with the issue of expropriations. This matter involved the armed robberies of companies and banks by the Bolsheviks in order to procure money for the Party.

This procedure had been ostracized by the 5th Congress because of its unscrupulous practices and its fears of detachment by local groups. Despite all these fears, the Bolsheviks continued in its unsavory ways.

In January of 1912, Lenin and some Mensheviks went ahead and got rid of their opposition from the party.

Trotsky, then, went ahead and organized a unification conference in Vienna in August 1912 called <u>The August Bloc.</u> This conference met, in retaliation, because of Lenin's conference which took place in Prague in January of 1912, where he ousted members of the party.

Trotsky became involved in another newspaper entitled, <u>Kievskaya Mysl</u> in which he became its war correspondent. He was sent to the Balkan Wars which he covered in September of 1912. It was during this time that he met Christian Rakovsky. They became friends and he and Christian worked for the Soviet Communist Party.

Then, on August 3rd, 1914, Trotsky fled from Vienna to Switzerland to avoid arrest as a Russian émigré. This incident was due to WWI which saw Austria-Hungary clash with Russian troops. The spark, which had ignited this conflagration, was the assassination of the Archduke Francis Ferdinand and his wife, Sophie, in Sarajevo, the capital of Bosnia.

At this time, the Party was split regarding their position in the war. Lenin, Martov, and Trotsky of the RSDLP (Revolutionary Socialist Democratic Liberation Party) advocated a policy of anti-war, while their opponents, Phekhanov, the Bolsheviks, and the Mensheviks supported the Russian government. Trotsky even wrote a book denouncing the war titled The War and the International.

Then, in November of 1914, Trotsky went to France and became a war correspondent for the newspaper, Kievskaya Mysl. Later, in 1915, in Paris, he edited a newspaper, the Nashe Slovo ("Our Word"), which was a socialist newspaper.

On March 31st, Trotsky was deported to Spain from France for anti-war remarks. The Spanish, not agreeing with his point of view, deported him on December 25th, 1916 to the United States. When he arrived in New York in January, 1917, he obtained several jobs writing for the newspapers. Novy Mir, a socialist newspaper, and the Der Forverts (The Forward) a Jewish daily language paper.

After being detained in Amherst, Nova Scotia for a month, he was finally released and made his way back to Russia in May.

At the First Congress of Soviets in June, he became a member of the Mezhraiontsy faction of the All-Russian Central Executive Committee.

Trotsky was elected chairman on October 8th after the Bolsheviks became the leading party in the Petrograd Soviet.

During this time, Trotsky took a leading part in the overthrow of the Kerensky Provisional Government.

Joseph Stalin, who was the General Secretary of the Communist Party, wrote in his book, The October Revolution, and stated infallibly, that Trotsky was the prime suspect in the Revolution of 1917.

By the end of 1917, Trotsky became, after Lenin, the second most important party member of the Bolsheviks. Trotsky became the People's Commissar for Foreign Affairs in the Party and the treaties which, at one time, had been signed by the Triple Entente, were now published by him.

Trotsky became involved with the peace negotiations from December 22nd, 1917 to February 10th, 1918, held in Brest-Litovsk where he was in charge of the Soviet delegation.

At that time, the Soviet government was split on several issues. On the Left, the Communists led by Nikolai Bukharin believed that a peace agreement between a capitalist country and a Soviet Republic could not be achieved. He felt that only a revolutionary war would bring a permanent peace to a Pan-European Soviet Republic.

Lenin, on the other hand, believed that Russia was too weak, militarily, to have an armed conflict with Germany and made arrangements with them to surrender providing he was placed in a powerful position as the Premier of Russia.

Trotsky's position was shaky and, he took a position between the two Bolshevik factions. However, he did agree with the Communist Left that a separate peace treaty with the Germans would cause an uproar and possibly a riot among the Russian people. Also, this agreement would have a tremendous effect on the morale and the material wealth of the government.

Nevertheless, because of Germany's strength, militarily, the Russian Bolshevik committee on February 18th, 1918, accepted Lenin's proposal for a peace agreement with Germany and sent a telegram to them accepting the terms of the Brest-Litovsk as stated.

This agreement was signed on March 3rd and ratified on March 15th, 1918. Because of his disagreement with this policy authored by the German government, Trotsky decided it was best for the Party that he resigns as the Commissar for Foreign Affairs.

After his resignation as Commissar for Foreign Affairs, he was appointed People's Commissar of Army and Navy Affairs, and also, chairman of the Supreme Military Council.

The post of commander-in-chief was done away with and Trotsky was placed in full charge of the Red Army which he enlarged and made a truly fighting machine, through measures of discipline, conscription, and the selection of officers on the basis of leadership rather than rank.

The Red Army increased in size under his rule from less than 300,000 to one million. He also introduced into the military, a group of Bolshevik political commissars whose function was to ensure the loyalty of these former Czar Officers.

In September of 1918, the military faced continuous difficulties and the government was forced to declare martial law; and also, reorganize the Red Army. The Supreme Military Council was disbanded and the position of commander-in-chief was reinstated.

Trotsky was given full authority over the military and became the chairman of the newly Revolutionary Military Council of the Republic.

Then, in September, Stalin and Trotsky again "banged heads" and disagreed with Trotsky's appointment of the former imperial general, Pavel Sytin, to command the Southern Front. Because of Stalin's refusal to accept the general's appointment, he was recalled from the front.

During the Red Army's battle with the White Army in 1919, the Red Army emerged the victor and was about to cross the Ural Mountains, when in the south, General Anton Denikin's White Russian Army made a calculated move and the Red Army's position became jeopardized.

The Central Committee, after their meeting, supported the generals of the Eastern Front, who wanted to capture Siberia before winter set in.

Because of his backing of Vatsetis, commander-in-chief and general of the Southern Front, Trotsky was criticized very vehemently by his opponents for his lack of leadership in this encounter.

Stalin, at this time, confronted Lenin to discharge Trotsky from his position. When Trotsky offered his resignation, it was rejected by the Central Committee and the Politburo.

After being sent to the Southern Front temporarily, Trotsky returned to Moscow and took control of the Red Army.

During the Civil War of 1919, Trotsky went to Petrograd to assist General Zinoviev and took part in the conflict, driving the army of Yudenich back to Estonia.

Because of his involvement in the conflict and his defense of Petrograd, Trotsky received the award of the Order of the Red Banner, a highly sought award.

After this conflict, Trotsky was assigned the task of restoring the economy of Russia in 1919 in the Ural region. Here, because of his proposal to abandon the economic policies of War Communism which included the confiscation of grain from the peasants and the restoration of the markets which dealt with the sale of grain, Lenin rejected this proposal and switched Trotsky's position to railroad commissioner.

It didn't take long for Lenin to see the "writing on the wall" for, in 1921, he witnessed the collapse of the economy and an uprising of the populace which forced him and the Bolshevik Party to accept the New Economic Policy and relinquish War Communism.

Then, in 1921, Lenin's health broke down and he became seriously ill. Between May 20th, 1922 and March 10th, 1923 he had three strokes which cause loss of speech, paralysis and finally death. His demise occurred on January 21st, 1924.

The position of General Secretary was formed by the Central Committee which Stalin assumed. So that Trotsky would not succeed Lenin, a troika (triumvirate) was formed.

Stalin and Trotsky became bitter rivals after Lenin's death. In 1925, Stalin had Trotsky ousted from his position as the Commissar of War. He then was expelled from the Central Committee in 1927 and, in 1929, was deported from the Soviet Union to Buyukada off the coast of Turkey. Later on, Daladier of France offered him asylum. His presence in France came to an abrupt end and, he was told that he was no longer welcomed there. He was given permission by Trygve Lie to enter Norway. Because of pressure from Russia, he was told to leave in 1936. From here, he boarded a freighter which took him to Mexico where he was greeted with open arms by Mexican President Lazaro Cardenas. He was transported from the Port of Tampico to Mexico City.

For a while, he stayed at the home of the painter, Diego Rivera and his wife, Frida Kahlo. After a disagreement with the family, he moved his residence to Avenida Viena in May, 1939.

While he was encamped at this villa, he came in contact with Joseph Hansen, Farrell Dobbs, and James P. Cannon who were affiliated with the Socialist Workers Party in the United States and did some work with them.

Later, Trotsky became ill and suffered from high blood pressure. He even contemplated suicide.

After writing a document on February 27th, 1940, in which he thanked his wife, Natalia Sedova, and his friends for their loyal support, he survived a raid at his home by three Stalinist assassins on May 24th, 1940.

Then on August 20th, 1940, he received the coup-de-grace when a Russian GPU agent, Ramon Mercader, who had seduced Sylvia Agelof a New Yorker supporter of Trotsky, and who had introduced him to the Trotsky household, approached Trotsky while he was feeding his pet rabbits. Mercader had hidden an ice ax under his raincoat which he was carrying and presented to Trotsky an article which he prompted him to read. As Trotsky sat down in his study to read the article, he was suddenly attacked by Mercader who struck him in the head with the ice ax. As Mercader tried to hit him a second time, Trotsky grabbed the assailant's arm and bit it, hoping his adversary would drop the lethal weapon.

The guards at the villa, hearing the screams of Trotsky, immediately disarmed Mercader and severely beat him. Both parties were rushed to the hospital where Trotsky died. Mercader was sentenced to 20 years in prison. After an investigation, it was learned that Leonid Eitingon, alias General Kotov, a Kremlin agent, was in charge of the assassination.

In 1987, President Gorbachev stated that Trotsky was a "hero and martyr." Then, in 1989, Trotsky's books, which had been forbidden, were finally published in the Soviet Union.

Today, Trotsky is regarded as a staunch Bolshevik and a supporter of Lenin, and especially, of the October Revolution of 1917. He was a leader of the Red Army and an orthodox Marxist. He believed in an international "permanent revolution" in contrast to that of Lenin, who favored the theory of Socialism in One Country which Trotsky firmly rejected. Trotsky and his supporters of the Fourth International thoroughly disagreed most vehemently with Stalin's philosophy of totalitarianism. They advocated that political revolutions needed democracy in order for socialism to survive.

The legacy which Trotsky has left for society is very limited—economic sustenance for the poor peasants, restoration of markets, better working conditions for industrial workers and, his defiance and vehemence for Stalin's totalitarian doctrines.

MOHANDAS KARAMCHAND "MAHATMA" GANDHI—1948

MAHATMA GANDI IS REMEMBERED IN history as the man who instigated reforms of nonviolence to accomplish resistance to political and social injustice that was ripe during Britain's occupation of India.

Gandhi was born on October 2nd, 1869 at Porbandar in British occupied India. He was the son of the prime minister to the maharajah of the state of Porbandar. His mother belonged to the Jainist religion which was immersed in a vegetarian diet.

To give their son a decent education they sent him to England in 1882 to study law. When he graduated, he went to Bombay in 1891 and later to South Africa until 1914 to practice his lawyer skills.

In 1915, he returned to India and became involved with the nationalist movement whose goal was the independence of India, especially, after he learned of the massacre of hundreds of nationalists by British troops at Amristar in 1919.

Because of this cauldron of human waste and suffering, Gandhi emerged as a leader of the Indian National Congress.

It is interesting to note that at this time he began to wear clothes which the "untouchables" (India's lowest social class) wore. He even preached that his followers weave their own cloth and soon the spinning wheel's use grew by leaps and bounds and eventually became the Insignia of Congress and was placed on the Indian flag.

All was not bad under British rule. The British raj (rule) had brought a whole host of reforms. India became more unified than ever before. It did away with civil war, banditry, and even the outlandish custom of suttee in which a widow was burned to death on her husband's funeral pyre.

The British administration there was admirable and efficient. Even other governments copied the British techniques of administration. The Britons improved public health and reduced famine by operating great irrigation projects and by increasing a network of railroads which made it possible to ship food to areas which were at one time inaccessible. Even the courts were improved in administering justice.

To quote a passage from Theodore Roosevelt in which he praises the British administration of India: "The successful administration of the Indian Empire has been one of the most notable and most admirable achievements of the white race during the past two centuries" shows the admiration of the British government for their concern and welfare of the Indian people.

Despite all these achievements, the Indians became more violent and restive under the British law (raj). As a result, in 1859, a mutiny occurred in which native troops (sepoys) emerged because of the indifference shown by the British toward India's religious customs.

Even the economy of India took a downfall as the British took measures of keeping low Indian tariffs in order to open up markets for manufacture goods made in England.

In civil service, the British gave the Indians lower positions and prevented them from obtaining commissions in the army.

Also, the British organized a Western curriculum in the universities that they established for the Indian populace.

To emphasize this prejudice and arrogance, Thomas Macaulay, the English historian who had assisted in the development of the Indian university curriculum showed this cultural arrogance by stating: "a single shelf of a good European library was worth the whole native literature of India and Arabia."

Gandhi felt that the British rule (raj) was "a crime against humanity . . . perhaps unequaled in history."

To stop this arrogance he proposed techniques of nonviolent resistance. This technique of nonviolence emanated mainly from Indian religious tradition and partly from the Christian Bible.

He also extracted these thoughts and ideas from his readings of Leo Tolstoy, and Henry David Thoreau. His philosophy centered on love of the Christian doctrine "love thy neighbor as thyself." He preached that his followers should show love of the British even though they didn't have to cooperate with them. He, however, defied British law and organized a boycott of all British institutions. Because of this action, he and thousands of his followers went to prison. Then, in 1930, he forged a new satyagraho (truth force) against the salt tax that resulted in the arrest of more than 60,000 Indians. He then campaigned for rural education and the elimination of the lingering sore of untouchability placed on the lower class of Indian society.

He and his friend, Jawaharlal Nehru demanded immediate independence. They, then, invoked a plan of non-cooperation by issuing a slogan titled, "Quit India." This, in turn, aggravated the British authorities and Gandhi and his cohort, Nehru, plus thousands of other Congressional leaders, found themselves in jail. This incarceration resulted in arson, mutinies of native troops, strikes of employees, and other bedlams. People took to the streets attacking European civilians and demanded independence.

In 1945, the Labor Party secured a momentous victory and this, in turn, resulted in a change of attitude toward the Indian proposal for independence.

Therefore, the British government was finally ready to accept terms for independence. However, this was bottled up in religious matters between the "hard-nosed" Moslems and Hindus.

The Congress wanted a single Indian state but this suggestion was botched by the Moslem League who demanded a separate state, Pakistan, because of the Moslem majority in the provinces located in the east and northwest.

The Moslems won out and in August of 1947, the British relinquished their authority to the two new states—Pakistan and India.

However, peace was yet to be accomplished for, independence was followed by a hemophiliac outburst between the Moslems and the Hindus. It has been estimated that hundreds of thousands of women, children, and men were slaughtered. Refugees numbered in the millions.

Gandhi was horrified about this religious tragedy. So, in 1948, he began a fast that lasted for several days declaring that he would continue to do so until death unless the Hindus stopped killing the Moslems.

The result of his effort proved positive as the leaders promised that the Moslem property, mosques, and most important, their lives, would be spared.

However, after this promise came to fruition on January 30th, 1948, a Hindu assassinated Gandhi who had the mistaken belief that Gandhi was in favor of the Moslem religion.

A man's illustrious career was terminated before his idea came to fruition. He believed that changes in society could be made by taking non-violent action. This idea did bear fruit later when another great leader, Martin Luther King believed in the achievement of civil rights by using this same method of non-violence.

FAISAL II OF IRAQ—1958

FAISAL WAS THE ONLY SON of Iraq's second king, Ghazi I and his wife Queen Aliya. When Faisal was just three years old, his father was killed in a car crash. Abdal-Ilah, his uncle, served as Regent until Faisal came of age in 1953. Faisal was born in Baghdad on May 2nd, 1935. At the early age, he was tutored at the royal palace. He attended Harrow-School in the United Kingdom with his cousin King Hussein of Jordan when he was a teenager.

The boys had planned to merge their two kingdoms because of military Arab nationalism which threatened their kingdoms. This action and that taken by his regent, Abdal-Ilah, to permit Great Britain's role in Iraqi transactions through the Baghdad Pact of 1955, and the Anglo-Iraqi Treaty of 1948, led to his eventual "demise".

Because of these pacts, people rose up in protest which resulted in hundreds of deaths and an adverse outlook on the imperial crown.

Then, in 1952, Faisal decided to visit the United States where he was greeted by the President, Harry Truman. He, also, met other celebrities—Dean Acheson, the famous Dodger ball player Jackie Robinson, and the famous British actor, James Mason.

Faisal's political activities commenced on May 2nd, 1953. Immediately, he ran into trouble because of his lack of administrative experience and his run in with a Pan-Arab nationalist group of sympathizers.

His reign was jeopardized not only from outside political groups, but also, from him and his ministers' miscalculations in their administration of governmental activities. Eventually, these serious mistakes led to his down fall.

Despite the political advice from his uncle and General Nuri al-Sa'ed, who had been the Prime Minister for several terms, Faisal's regime took a set-back politically in 1950, when the king and his top advisors decided to invest their wealth in the development of oil projects. The result of this transaction increased the hostility of the peasantry and the middle class as it widened the gap between the two classes. Another thorn in the side of the peasantry was the control of parliament by the upper classes. Reformists thought that the only solution to this dilemma was a revolution. The downfall of Egypt's monarchy in 1952 by Gamul Abdel Nasser was the spark which ignited the movement of the reformists.

When Syria joined Egypt in February of 1958, after Nasser's takeover of the regime forming the United Arab Republic, Jordan and Iraq decided to form an alliance which would safeguard and strengthen their relationship.

Then, on February the 14th, this relationship became the Arab Federation of Iraq and Jordan with Faisal as the head of state. Unfortunately, this alliance, after a period of five months, came officially to an abrupt end.

The Faisal regime took a quick turn in 1956 during Israel's war with Egypt and the nationalization of the Suez Canal by Nasser. The regime's popularity deteriorated and the situation became grave when the Baghdad Pact was denounced by an aggravated citizenry.

Groups began to organize in defiance to the administration's wrong-doings.

In February, 1957, a group was organized called a "Front of National Union" which unified the objectives of the Communists, Independents, and the Ba'th parties and coordinated the various activities of these individual groups.

The regime tried to preserve the loyalty of the military by offering it various benefits. An Iraqi officer group organized as the "Supreme Committee of Free Officers" became anti-monarchy in their political views and activities.

In 1958, during the crisis in Lebanon, King Hussein of Jordan requested military aid from Iraq. However, General Ab al-Karim Qasim did a switch. Instead of marching to Jordan, he changed his mind, and instead, went to Baghdad where he engaged in a coup d'état on July 14th, 1958.

Then, during the "14 July Revolution," Faisal surrendered to the insurgents offering no resistance. Captain Abdul Sattar Sabaa Al-Ibousi who led the assault at the palace told the King and his relatives to congregate in the palace courtyard. After being told to face a wall, they were brutally mowed down by machine gun fire. Faisal did not immediately die from the attack but, on the way to a hospital, he succumbed. On the following day, Faisal's Prime Minister, Nuri as-Said, was also brutally murdered by Quassim's henchmen.

The control of Iraq was passed to a tripartite, "Sovereignty Council," composed of representatives of three ethnic groups. The Ba'th party finally took over in 1963 followed by the reign of Saddam Hussein that villainous dictator who brought on the Desert War by invading the small country of Kuwait.

An incident which is worth mentioning was the Anglo-Iraqi War begun in 1940 which pitted England against its formidable foe, Iraq. The prime minister of Iraq at the time, was Rashid 'Ali' Al. The reason for the confrontation with Britain was because of its relations with Germany and Italy. The British forced Rashid out in January 1941, but he was brought back in a semi coup in April. He was forced to flee to Iran in May, 1941, and he later fled to Saudi Arabia and then to Egypt. He was also involved in a Nasirite plot and was given the death sentenced. He was eventually pardoned for this involvement and went into exile in Lebanon and then Egypt. This was his final role in the political arena.

Besides this achievement, nothing else can be ascribed to Faisal's government. He didn't promote the status of the peasantry but increased the wealth of the upper classes—the elite, landowners and his fellow supporters. After considering the failures of his administration, his rating as a monarch is practically nil.

RAFAEL TRUJILLO OF THE DOMINICAN REPUBLIC—1961

TRUJILLO WAS THE SON OF Jose Trujillo Valdez and Altagracia Julia Molina Chevalier later known as Mama Julia. He was born and raised in San Cristobal. His real name was Rafael Leonidas Trujillo Molina. He was the third of eleven children and related to the Abreus family.

Trujillo was regarded as a lady's man for, he was married four times—to Aminta Ledesma from his hometown of San Cristobal, to Bienvenida Ricardo a girl from Montecristi, to Maria de los Angeles Matinez, and last but not least, to Lina Lovaton Pittaluga who was a debutante from the upper-class. He had two brothers José Arismendy who saw the creation of the main radio station (La Voz Dominicans), which later became the television station, and Hector, who also held a position in the government.

Trujillo's education was limited to a certain degree. When he was only six years old, he attended the school of Hilario Merino. Later, he enrolled at the school of Broughton and stayed there for a period of four years. Here, he was regarded by his professors as being unintelligent.

At the age of sixteen, he worked as a Morse code telegraph operator. It was during this time that he joined a gang titled "The 44" based in Dominica. In 1916 he procured a job in a sugar industry as "camp guard." In the same year, the United States, because of threats of defaults by the Dominican island regarding their foreign debts, took over the island. It was during this occupation that the United States had established an army constabulary to contain order there. While there, Trujillo gained recognition as a recruiter and worked his way up the ranks and was eventually promoted. When the United States vacated the island in 1924, Trujillo was put in charge.

A rebellion took place in Santiago in 1930 led by Rafael Estrella against President Vasquez. Vasquez was forced to resign and Estrella took his place as president. Then, in the 1930 presidential election, Trujillo became the nominee of the new political party of Dominica. Because he received an unbelievable amount of votes, the election was declared fraudulent by a judge. Because of this accusation, he was forced to flee the country.

When he returned, he took over the reins of government as a virtual dictator.

On August 16, 1931, Trujillo made the Dominican Party the only legal political party of the country. Trujillo forced government employees to give 10 percent of their salary to the national treasury. He, also, required members of the party to carry a membership card and, if they didn't have the card on their person when they were confronted, they could be arrested for vagrancy. Trujillo, in order to secure his authority, had his opponents killed.

In 1934, he promoted himself as the General of the Army. At this time, he was up for re-election which was a total farce as there was only one party. The election was a mere formality. Citizens swore loyalty to him through the process of "civic reviews."

Trujillo's administration turned out to be a hilarious circus. First of all, the capital of Santo Domingo was renamed Ciudad Trujillo by their Congress in 1936. Second, the province of San Cristobal was named as "Trujillo." Third, Pico Duarte, the nations highest peak was renamed in his honor. Fourth, statues of "El Jefe," his pseudonym, were stationed all across the Republic. Fifth, public buildings were erected to praise him. He had an electric sign constructed in Ciudad Trujillo so that the slogan "Dios y Trujillo" could be seen at night.

To show his hypocrisy, he had stated that he would limit his position only as the Generalissimo of the army and refuse the presidential appointment in the election of 1938; then, he reversed himself in 1942 when he ran for re-election as president and won easily. Because he served two terms, he had to lengthen the term as president to five years. His brother, Hector, became the nominal president in 1952.

Trujillo gained a substantial reputation because of his open-door policy. He granted asylum to Jews from Europe, exiles from Spain following their civil war in 1936, and also, the Japanese migration of 1930.

In 1940, Trujillo donated 26,000 acres of his land for settlements for these refugees. The Trujillo government favored mostly Caucasian refugees over all the others and he used this numerical increase in population to increase taxes. The troops of the Republic were told to expel illegal aliens. This action by the Dominican military resulted in the 1937 Parsley Massacre of Haitian immigrants.

In his foreign policy, he tended to lean with the United States in its condemnation of Communism. On December 11th, 1941, he joined the Allies and declared war on Japan and Germany. While the country did not physically partake in the war, it did, however, become a founding member of the United Nations.

Trujillo's wish was to have closely knit ties with the United States, economically and diplomatically. Because of his brutality, assassination attempts and killings, he was ostracized by other nations. The United States relationship with him slowly deteriorated. Because of his fear of other nations, he had a tendency to give special attention to the military. He gave them generous pay increases and various perks besides increasing their fire power with more arms.

Trujillo was able to increase his and his family's wealth by establishing state monopolies over various enterprises throughout the country.

He also negotiated a treaty with Cordell Hull in 1936, whereby, the United States terminated its position as the administrator of Dominican customs and finances with the provision that the Dominican Republic repay its debts.

In 1937, Trujillo had difficulties with Haiti which shared the island with the Dominican Republic. The Haitians had constantly encroached on them so, Trujillo met the Haitian President, Stenio Vincent, hoping to solve the problems which had existed at the border. This meeting proved advantageous for, in 1936, a settlement was reached. At the same time, the notorious Trujillo was organizing a plot to overthrow the Vincent government of Haiti.

After several incursions at the border, Trujillo initiated the Parsley Massacre in which thousands of Haitians were slaughtered. Haiti eventually called for an international investigation. Because of increase pressure from the United States government, Trujillo agreed to a reparation settlement in January, 1938, which involved a great deal of money to the survivors and the victims of the holocaust.

Trujillo also had trouble with Castro's Cuba. They wished to overthrow his regime and it tried to do so on June 14th, 1959. However, it was foiled in its attempt. Then, in August 1959, Johnny Abbes, a leader of the secret police, SIM, plotted to eliminate Castro. His group landed at Trinidad, Cuba but his attempt to assassinate Castro was foiled when Castro's troops surrounded the plane.

As Trujillo engaged in the domestic affairs with other countries, his reputation was diminished. He personally hated the president of Venezuela, Romulo Betancourt, who had plotted with Dominicans to overthrow him. Trujillo, in turn, plotted with exiles from Venezuela to oust him in retaliation. The Venezuelan government finally took action against Trujillo and appealed to the OAS (Organization of American States) because of his interference in the affairs of their government. In retaliation, Trujillo ordered his foreign agents to plant a bomb in Betancourt's car. However, this explosion did not kill Betancourt but injured him. Again, because of this horrific incident, Trujillo loss respect worldwide.

The OAS did impose economic sanctions on the Dominican Republic, and also, severed diplomatic relations with the governments. The United States government finally realized that the relationship with Trujillo was causing a hardship and embarrassment with other countries, especially, after the Betancourt incident, and also, after the brutal murder of the three Mirabal sisters in November 25th, 1960.

All these savage incidents were finally exposed and showed the true nature of Trujillo's personality—egotistical, paranoid, secretive, methodical, energetic, extravagant in dress, and no friends to speak of except associates with whom he did business with. Because of his cruelty and harsh treatment of people, on the night of May 30th, 1961, he was ambushed as his car traveled on San Cristobal Avenue in Santo Domingo. His body was riddled with machine-gun fire.

The de la Maza family had been accused as the main instigator in the plot because of Trujillo's execution of their son.

However, an internal CIA memorandum stated that an Office of Inspector General investigation disclosed that the Agency did take a central part in the assassination. Trujillo's son Ramfis retrieved his father's body from the grave located in his hometown of San Cristobal and relocated it in Paris at the Pire Lachaise Cemetery at the request of his relatives.

His legacy shows his thirst for power, money, fame, clothing, and also, his sexual appetite for pretty women. It has been estimated that his wealth was staggering, in the millions of dollars at the time of his death, and that he had accumulated over 111 companies of various sorts which he and his family operated.

An unhappy end came to a tyrant who was hated by his fellow man and the world around him.

MEDGAR EVERS—1963

MEDGAR WILEY EVERS WAS BORN in Decatur, Mississippi on July 2nd, 1925. His father was James Evers and his mother Jessie Evers. He was the fourth child of six children of the Evers' family. He married a classmate, Myrlie Beasley on December 24th, 1951, while attending Alcorn State University and they had three children, two boys and a girl.

His education was limited in his childhood for, in 1943, he decided to quit school and he dropped out of the 10th grade. Later, he and his brother, Charlie, decided to enlist in the army and both saw action during WWII in France. He was honorably discharged in 1945 and had worked his way up the ladder in the service and became a Sergeant. In 1946, he and his brother returned home. For his participation in the war, he received two bronze stars. While attending Alcorn State University, he was very active in sports and other activities—football and track, the debating team, sang in the choir, and became the junior class president.

After collage, he and his wife moved to Mound Bayou, Mississippi. There, he was hired by T.R.M. Howard to sell insurance for his company, the Magnolia Mutual Life Insurance. While there, Medgar became involved in an activist group which pushed for civil rights for blacks. The organization was called the Regional Council of Negro Leadership and the president was Howard. One of their activities involved the boycott of service stations which didn't permit blacks to use their restrooms. Medgar had spearheaded this boycott.

Annual conferences were held in Mound Bayou between 1952 and 1954 which Medgar attended.

Later, trouble brewed when he applied to the segregated Law School at the University of Mississippi. His application was rejected because he was black. As a result, the NAACP (National Association for the Advancement of Colored People) led a campaign in which Evers was the key object in the fight for the entrance of black students to the University. This case finally reached the United States Supreme Court.

Medgar became the state field secretary for the NAACP for nine years.

Then, on June 11th, 1963, because of his involvement in the black civil rights movement, he was ambushed and shot in the back and killed when he left his car and walked up to his home in Jackson, Mississippi.

Governor Ross Barnett didn't exude any emotions after he heard about this horrific incident; his reply was simply, "apparently it was a dastardly act."

President John. F. Kennedy and his brother Robert, Attorney General, denounced officials in Mississippi for not taking any action in the killing. They, in turn, were highly criticized for lack of action on the civil rights crises.

The FBI stepped in and investigated the assassination. They found a fertilizer salesman by the name of Byron de la Beckwith who was a member of the Citizens Council of Mississippi, guilty of the murder. They had found a telescopic rife with his fingerprints on the rifle near Ever's home. In order to pay for Beckwith's legal fees, a White Citizens Legal Fund was initiated in Beckwith's hometown of Greenwood.

Because of all white juries during the two trials, Beckwith was found not guilty. However, in 1994, when a jury composed of eight blacks and four whites heard the new evidence, they convicted him of murder and he was sentenced to life imprisonment.

It was not until the Johnson administration in 1965 that laws were enacted giving more civil rights to blacks.

Finally, justice did prevail in Jackson, Mississippi and Medgar's efforts did prevail in the overturn of the segregated laws in the South.

NGO DINH DIEM—FIRST PRESIDENT
OF THE REPUBLIC OF VIETNAM—1963

DIEM WAS BORN ON JANUARY 3rd, 1901 at Hue, French Indochina. He was unmarried and was a Roman Catholic. The third of six sons, Diem was christened Jean-Baptiste. He and his family were converted to Catholicism in the 17th century by Portuguese missionaries.

His family came from a lower class of citizenry until his father passed the imperial examinations which gave them a boost economically. During the French colonization of Vietnam, his father, Ngo Dinh Kha became a mandarin and counselor to the emperor, Thanh Thai after negating his choice to become a Catholic priest. Kha decided to become a farmer in 1907 when the French deposed the emperor on the grounds of insanity because of his constant bickering of French colonization.

While attending a French Catholic school, Diem worked, in his free time, in his father's rice fields. His father, later on, opened up a private school which he attended.

After entering a monastery (he followed his elder brother Ngo Dinh Thuc there), he found it too debilitating and left. While attending a French lyceum in Hue he was accepted because of his high grades in their examinations. He was then offered a scholarship to Paris which he declined. The reason he forfeited this scholarship was because he wanted to become a priest. Again, because of the difficulty of the agenda, he reneged. Not yet satisfied with his educational desires, he embarked on a journey to Hanoi where he enlisted at the School of Public Administration and Law. This French school specialized in the training of Vietnamese bureaucrats.

All of this education paid off for, in 1921, he graduated at the top of his class. He, then, joined the civil service "taking a pitch" from his elder brother, Ngo Dinh Khoi, who, also, had become a civil service employee.

During this sojourn, he rose in rank from mandarin to higher positions. His promotions accumulated rapidly—he served in Hue at the library; he became the district chief of seventy villages; and later, he was promoted as provincial chief presiding over 300 villages. His rise in status was enhanced by his relationship with Nguyen Huu Bai who was the Catholic head of the Council of Ministers, and also, the father of the daughter who married Diem's brother, Khoi.

Later on, he became involved in anti-communist activities. His interest in this involvement took place while he was riding a horse through the area near Quang Tri when he noticed people handing out leaflets of communist propaganda.

He was given a promotion of governorship of the Phan Thiet Province in 1929 for his involvement in the capture of communist instigators. Then, in 1931, with the assistance of French forces, he suppressed a communist revolt. The communists went on a rampage, raping and murdering innocent civilians.

In 1933, with the ascendancy of Bao Dai to the throne, Diem was appointed by the French to be his interior minister. After serving for three months in this position, Diem resigned; his excuse was the refusal by the French to introduce a Vietnamese legislature which he had recommended.

Because of his actions, he was threatened with arrest and his title was confiscated.

For his punishment, he was not to have a prestigious job for twenty years. During this lull in his life, he engaged himself in various activities, such as, attending church, hunting, reading, and photography.

During WWII, he tried to obtain the independence of Vietnam in 1942 by negotiating with the occupied Japanese forces but, to no avail.

It was during this lapse of negotiations with the Japanese that Diem found a secret political party called the Association for the Restoration of Great Vietnam. The French became aware of the association's existence in 1944 and declared that he was a subversive and arrested him. In disguising himself as a Japanese officer, he was able to avoid his capture and fled to Saigon, unharmed.

Then, in 1945, he declined the premiership of a puppet regime under Bao Dai offered by the Japanese. However, he later tried to reclaim this offer, but unfortunately, Bao Dai had already given the position to someone else.

After the Japanese withdrew from Vietnam in September of 1945, Ho Chi Minh took over and announced the Democratic Republic of Vietnam and commenced a brutal war with the French.

On Diem's way to Hue to try to convince Bao not to join Ho, he was arrested by the Vietminh and exiled to a village in the highlands.

Here, he contacted several diseases and if it were not for the care he received from local tribesmen, he would have died.

After a period of approximately six months, he traveled to Hanoi to meet Ho. He was asked by him to join the Vietminh but he refused because of the death of his brother Khoi who had been buried alive by the Vietminh soldiers.

Ho ordered Diem's arrest because he continually propagated anti-communist reform which Ho resented. However, Diem gained a respite in November when the French and the Vietminh engaged in a major war.

During this time, Diem moved to Saigon to live with his elder brother, Ngo Dinh Thuc. Diem and his brothers jointly founded the Vietnam National Alliance. Its purpose was to obtain dominion status for Vietnam by the French. The French asked Diem to lobby for Bao Dai and to join them. Diem felt that Dai's deal with the French was not sufficient, so he returned to Hue.

It was during this transaction that Bao Dai offered Diem the position of Prime Minister which he refused. Then, in 1950, the Vietminh became very irritated over Diem's activities denouncing communism, so they sentenced him to death in his absence.

While traveling to the Mekong Delta to visit his brother Thuc, Ho's soldiers tried to kill him. Diem, then, in 1950, left Vietnam and got permission from the French to travel to Rome to participate in the Holy Year celebrations at the Vatican.

Before this visit to Rome, he proceeded to Japan to seek authority from Cuong De. He, also, tried to obtain an audience with General Douglas MacArthur who was the American Supreme Commander there. These meetings with the two administrators didn't materialize.

However, a friend of Diem did help to arrange a meeting with Wesley Fishel who had previously did work for the United States government as a consultant. Fishel was against colonialism and communism in Asia, and therefore, was a proponent of Diem's ideas. Fishel helped to arrange meetings with the U.S. Acting Secretary of State, James Webb. Because of his poor performance with United States officials, he loss contact with them. In 1951, Diem was able to secure an interview with Secretary of State, Dean Acheson. He, also, met Cardinal Francis Spellman who was a friend of his archbishop brother, Thuc. They both had studied in Rome. Because of the relationship with his brother, Cardinal Spellman arranged a meeting for Diem with Pope Pius XII.

Cardinal Spellman assisted Diem in gaining political support among Catholics and the right wing in America.

Diem, while taking a tour in the eastern part of the United States, spoke at several universities where he felt he could trump up support for his future campaign. Here, he emphasized the fact "that Vietnam could only be saved for the 'free world' if the United States sponsored a government of nationalists who were opposed to both the Vietminh and the French."

Because of his popularity and determination to defeat communism in Vietnam, he was appointed as a consultant to Michigan State University's Government Research Bureau. Fishel worked here and its purpose was to administer government-sponsored assistance programs for cold war allies.

Diem gained a great deal of support in America in contrast to the decline of the French support in Vietnam.

In 1954, the Vietminh, under the leadership of Ho Chi Minh, captured Dien Bien Phu. Because of this Vietminh victory, the French lost control of Vietnam.

Realizing Diem's popularity among American diplomats, Bao Dai chose Diem's youngest brother, Ngo Dinh Luyen to be part of his delegation at the 1954 Geneva Conference. This meeting was held to determine the future of Indochina. The Geneva Accords had stated that Vietnam was to be partitioned temporarily at the 17th parallel. The intent of the elections of 1956 was to reunify the country.

Bao Dai, during this period, named Diem as the Prime Minister with the support of President Dwight D. Eisenhower. Diem, as Prime Minister, controlled the French supported State of Vietnam in the South while the Vietminh controlled the North.

With the French collapse of Indochina in 1955 due to the Vietminh victory, Diem's delegation of the South did not sign the Geneva Accords, because they did not want the country split in two with the communists in control in the North.

Nevertheless, the agreement went into effect despite the delegation's disagreement. Because of this division, many Catholics in the North were forced to migrate to the southern zone. Diem, being a Catholic, greeted these Catholics with open arms. The United States government lent a hand in the migration by using a Navy program, Operation Passage to Freedom, which shuttled up to one million North Vietnamese, South. Most of these migrants were Catholic. Edward Lansdale, a CIA agent, helped Diem in this operation by providing a propaganda campaign which enticed the refugees to move south. This propaganda was used also to frighten the population of the North of the disasters which would await them if they didn't move South.

Diem's popularity at this time was diminished. The French hated him; Bao disliked him; and two religious sects, the Cao and Hoa Hao, opposed his views.

Besides all this hostility, Diem had another grave problem. In the capital, Binh Xuyen was the head of a crime syndicate which included an army of 40,000. He controlled an organization of vice which included casinos, opium factories, and brothels. He even had control of the police. Emperor Bao Dai had given Binh this control for the enormous pay off of 1.25 million United States dollars. This enormous power placed Diem in an awkward position where his authority was limited and his control was contained about his palace grounds.

Then, in August, Diem was attacked by an avalanche of propaganda by his archenemy, General Nguyen Van Hinh, Chief of Staff and a French citizen declaring Diem to be a weak and incompetent leader. He, also, stated that he was preparing a coup against Diem. However, this did not gain momentum because of the efforts of Diem's friend of the CIA, Lansdale who arranged holidays for Hinh's officer. Despite the collapse of this ugly attempt to get rid of Diem, the French persisted in their efforts to destabilize his government and debase his popularity.

In 1955, after the defeat of the French at the Battle of Dien Bien Phu, the French withdrew from Indochina. This left Diem in temporary control of the South. An election was held in October of 1955 to determine the South's political position. Bao, the Emperor, wanted a monarchy while Diem wanted a republic for Vietnam. Ngo Dinh Nhu, Diem's brother, supervised and organized the election. However, the election was rigged—Bao's campaigning was prevented and besides, his supporters were attacked by Nhu's cohorts. Diem's tally showed an exceedingly amount of fraud as the number of votes didn't coincide with the number of registrants.

Under the 1954 Geneva Accords, Vietnam was to have elections in 1956 to reunite the country. Diem canceled these claiming that South Vietnam was not affiliated with the convention. He, also, criticized the communists for the lack of freedom in such affairs. Nevertheless, the elections were to be held in August, 1959, due to pressure exerted on him by the United States and mainly, his own country. The election would also choose a national legislature.

Diem, again, took drastic action to oppose the opposition and to "bury" the candidates, politically. "He prohibited political meetings which exceeded five people; he didn't allow the newspapers to publish the names of independent candidates." Even in the rural areas he put the "clamp" on candidates who ran for office by charging them with conspiracy with the Vietcong. For these charges, a penalty of death was imposed.

Phan Quang Dan, a notorious critic of the government was allowed to run for office. Despite various means undertaken by Diem to quell his support in the voting, Dan still managed to obtain enough votes to claim a victory. Unfortunately, he was arrested when the new assembly convened. These incidents indicate the immense corruption which existed in Diem's government.

Diem's administration was riddled with fraud, indifference, cruelty, and nepotism. His brothers obtained an immense fortune through graft and corruption. His brother Nyo Dinh Nhu was a staunch admirer of Adolf Hitler and was, also, an opium addict. Diem placed his younger brother, Ngo Dinh Can in charge of the former Imperial City of Hue. His other brother, Ngo Dinh Luyen was given the post as Ambassador to the United Kingdom. Last, but not least, was his elder brother Ngo Dinh Thuc who became the archbishop of Hue and a friend of Cardinal Spellman.

His brothers' positions prove the widespread nepotism which existed during Diem's rule.

In addition to these positions, the brothers obtained, as previously mentioned, an enormous fortune and became millionaires as they garnered money through graft, smuggling, and monopolizing trade in the cinnamon industry. In order to cover up this amassed fortune, they stored the money in foreign banks.

Since Diem wasn't married, his brother's wife, Madame Nhu became the First Lady of South Vietnam. She and Diem went on a personal crusade to eliminate the corruption which existed under Binh Xuyen who had organized a crime syndicate under Bao Dai and the French government.

In Saigon, she and Diem went ahead and closed brothels and opium dens. They, also, made divorce and abortion illegal and strengthened the laws of adultery. Diem went ahead and broke up the armies of the Cao Dai and Hoa Hao religious sects of the Mekong Delta.

Because of his animosity toward the communists, Diem went on a rampage by killing anyone who was suspected of being a communist. He had at least 75,000 imprisoned and an estimate of 50,000 slain. This slaughter didn't stop here. He, also, killed anti-communist dissidents and informers of anti-corruption.

In 1957, Diem's power began to recede and a spirit of insurgency developed throughout country. In January of 1959, the Hanoi Central Committee took action by issuing a secret decree which authorized the use of force in the South.

In December, 1960, Hanoi gave permission to the southern communists to establish the National Front for the Liberation of South Vietnam. This edict was formed for the sole purpose of getting rid of the government of the South.

This organization was composed of two groups: intellectuals of South Vietnam who opposed the government and were nationalists and, the other who were composed of communists who remained in the South after the partition. In addition there were those from the northern zone which included a peasant class from local areas.

In order to confront this political party of communists from the North, Diem took action by instituting an insurgency group titled the Strategic Hamlet Program. This organization called for the consolidation of 14,000 villages of South Vietnam into 11,000 hamlets. The purpose of founding this organization was to counteract and isolate the NLF (National Liberation Front) from the villages who were gathering information about Diem's government. Also, they were gathering supplies and recruiting soldiers who were a threat to Diem's government.

To attract world-wide attention to his needs and programs, Diem went on diplomatic visits to Australia and the United States. By visiting these two countries, he hoped to obtain support for his campaigns and to help these countries realize the threat that communism was imposing on the Southern government.

The attempt to assassinate Diem occurred several times. The first one occurred in 1960, and the second happened in 1962 when two air force officers bombed his palace.

Being a staunch Catholic and leaning to the consolidation of the Catholic Church, Diem, naturally, was very biased. The Buddhist comprised between 70 and 90 percent of the population and they were regarded as inferior. They were, therefore, given low or subservient positions in the government and the military. Buddhists were denied promotions in the army and were told to convert to Catholicism if they wished to be promoted.

Some Buddhist villages converted to Catholicism in order to avoid being resettled in other areas. Catholics enjoyed a wide supply of privileges. They were exempt from carvée labor which the government required of all citizens. The Catholic Church was exempt from property acquisition and the aid which came from the United States was given in large amounts to Catholic villages and less to the Buddhist communities. The universities of Dalat and Hue were under the jurisdiction of Catholic authorities.

Besides ignoring the needs of the Buddhist majority in South Vietnam, the government's relations with the United States worsened in 1963. This was due to several incidents which antagonized the Buddhists and brought attention to the United States.

Buddists were prohibited during the Vesak celebration from raising their flag which commemorated the birth of Gautama Buddha. Catholics, however, were given permission to fly their flags at one of their celebrations. This caused a great deal of enmity among the Buddhists. Thich Tri Quang, in retaliation for this bias, led a protest against the government which was squashed by Diem's forces and resulted in the killing of nine civilians. Diem, in a cover up, blamed the Vietcong for the deaths.

The Buddhists asked Diem for an agreement which consisted of five points. These were intended to promulgate their benefits with regard to government regulations. Diem called them "damn fools" for demanding such benefits, stating that they already had them. As a result of all this turmoil and protests, Diem went ahead and banned all demonstrations and told his police to arrest anyone found guilty of civil disobedience.

The outcome of these protests ended in several tragedies. The Buddhist monks, in protest of the infringement of the benefits of law, self-immolated which caught the attention of the United States.

Diem's brother, Nhu, who hated the Buddhists, staged a raid on the Xa Loi Pagoda in Saigon. The Pagodas were vandalized and the body of Thich Quang Duc was cremated. The monks were beaten most severely. The vandals demolished the statue of Gautama Buddha. These raids by Nhu's forces caused a widespread uprising throughout the country. Students at Saigon University boycotted their classes. The students at the Hue University did likewise. Even students in the high schools, demonstrated their feelings of contempt.

Vu Van Mau, Diem's foreign minister, shaved his head in protest. He resigned his office, was arrested and put in jail when he attempted to leave the country on a religious pilgrimage.

The United States finally realized the corruption and cruelty that Diem's regime was undergoing to safeguard their positions in government. The U.S. government decided to take more drastic action on his regime. President Kennedy told Henry Cabot Lodge, the Ambassador to South Vietnam, to refuse a meeting with Diem.

The United States government, after learning of a coup by the ARVN generals, instigated by General Duong Van Minh, gave its assurances of not meddling in their plot. With this assurance at hand, Minh and his cohorts overthrew Diem's regime on November 1st, 1963. At this time, the palace wasn't guarded proficiently, as only one guard was on duty. The conspirators were able to enter without provocation and confronted Diem and his younger brother, Ngo Dinh Nhu. They offered them safe escort out of the country if Diem agreed to surrender. Refusing this offer, Diem, his brother, and his entourage escaped by using an underground tunnel. Their destination was Cholon where they were taken into custody the following day. Their hands were tied and they were escorted to a vehicle which contained a tank corps major who had harsh words with Nhu. The major drew a dagger and stabbed Nhu repeatedly. He, then, drew his gun and shot Diem and his brother Nhu in the back of the head.

General Ton That Dinh was in charge of martial law in Saigon.

Dinh and his fellow officers tried to cover up the assassination by claiming that both of the brothers had committed suicide. Later on, this allegation was disclaimed as photos were taken which showed otherwise. Later, they changed their view and stated that they died accidentally. The brothers were buried in unmarked graves in a prison cemetery.

Madame Nhu accused America of instigating the demise of her husband, Nhu, and his brother, Diem.

The instigator of the coup, General Duong Van Minh, (known as "Big Minh") established a junta after the assassination but, he too loss power and fell into the depths of iniquity.

JOHN F. KENNEDY—1963

JOHN F. KENNEDY HAS GONE down in history as one of our great presidents. He has been noted for his courage, heroics, intelligence, determination, and his charismatic character.

Kennedy was born to a prominent Massachusetts Irish Catholic family in Brookline on May 29th, 1917. His father, Patrick Joseph Kennedy was an ambitious and ruthless politician who became a millionaire—some say by bootlegging.

He became very popular in political circles and was elected as an ambassador to Great Britain. His one ambition was to see one of his sons elected as president of the United States. This idea did come to fruition with the election of his son, John, in the 1960 election, when he ran against Richard M. Nixon of California who at that time was the Vice-President under President Dwight D. Eisenhower, the former U.S. General of the Allied Forces during WWII.

Kennedy won by a narrow margin over Nixon by fewer than 115,000 popular votes; however, in the Electoral College he pulled in 303 votes to 219 for Nixon.

During the four TV debates of the campaign, Kennedy showed more poise than Nixon when questioned by the panel. His personality and looks also had a great effect on the audience of on—lookers throughout the nation.

In his inaugural address, he defined the United States position in world affairs—stressing "common enemies"—disease, tyranny, poverty, and war. He also stressed that Russia and the United States should strive for peaceful solutions during the Cold War.

To his fellow Americans, he uttered his famous lines which have gone down in history as a plea for unity and posterity: "Ask not what

your country can do for you—ask what you can do for your country."
Smith, Carter. <u>Presidents—All You Need to Know</u>. Irvington, N.Y.: Hylas
Publishington, p. 224

Kennedy's earlier life was interesting and filled with accomplishments.
He attended various schools to obtain a good education, namely, Choate,
London School of Economics, Princeton University, Harvard University,
and Stanford University.

After he graduated from Harvard in 1940, he took on the task of
publishing his senior thesis titled: <u>Why England Slept</u> which was acclaimed
highly and became a best seller. Later, he wrote <u>Profiles in Courage</u> which
won the Pulitzer Prize for biography in 1957.

During WWII, he joined the Navy and was promoted to a captain and
was put in charge of a torpedo boat that was sunk by the Japanese in 1943.

It was at this time that Kennedy's reputation boomeranged and he
received plaudits for his heroism in saving his crew in the Pacific.

Because of his heroic action, he injured his back which had caused
him a great deal of pain throughout the remaining years of his life.

After his stint in the Navy, Kennedy decided to enter the political
arena. He was elected to the House of Representatives in 1947 under the
Democratic ticket and then, was projected to a seat in the Senate where he
ousted that stalwart Republican from Massachusetts, Henry Cabot Lodge,
in 1952. Then, in 1956, he made a bid for the vice-presidency. Failing to
achieve this position, he went on to run for the presidency of the United
States in the 1960 being elected as stated previously.

With the help of Lyndon B. Johnson, he was able to muster enough
votes for the presidency by taking the large state of Texas. Because of his
assistance, Kennedy appointed Johnson as his running mate.

At the age of 43, Kennedy was the youngest man ever elected to the
presidency and the only Catholic.

With his wife Jacqueline Lee Bouvier at his side, he reached great
heights during his administration. She served as an inspiration and advisor
to bolster his popularity and administration.

Kennedy's administration took some quick turns which at times were
good and sometimes bad.

For instance, the C.I.A. (United States Central Intelligent Agency)
persuaded Kennedy to support a landing of 1,500 armed Cuban refugees
at a place called the Bay of Pegs. It was hoped that the landing would set
off a rebellion in Cuban which, unfortunately, did not take place. Instead,

nearly the entire party was killed or captured. In order to secure the release of those who were captured, private donors in the United States gathered about $53 million in medicine and food which was given to Castro's government. Because of this failure, Castro still remained a Communist threat to the United States and it created a terrible embarrassment to the United States government and also weakened the Kennedy administration in the eyes of the world.

It has been said that this fiasco led to the Cuban Missile Crisis.

Nikita Khrushchev and Kennedy had met in Vienna in June of 1961. It was at this time that Khrushchev got the feeling that Kennedy was a weak man—emotionally that is. Therefore, he went ahead in building the Berlin Wall which divided Germany in two divisions—East and West. He also decided, with the approval of Castro, to install nuclear weapons in Cuba.

In October, 1962, the United States took aerial photographs which definitely showed rocket emplacements.

Kennedy took immediate action by imposing a naval blockade in Cuba.

Russian merchant ships were intercepted at sea on October 25th and turned around and headed home followed by United States planes to make sure they proceeded to Russian ports.

Then, on October 28th, 1962, Kennedy and Khrushchev reached an agreement whereby Russia would stop construction of missile bases in Cuba and remove all rockets there under United Nations supervision on condition that the United States promise not to invade Cuba.

In 1961, Kennedy had proposed an enormous amount of bills to strengthen the economy and promote civil rights in the South. This movement was called a "New Frontier."

He proposed that Congress legislate the following: federal aid to education, civil rights enactments, medical aid for the elderly, and a build-up of the space program. However, he wasn't successful with these proposals for, many southern democratic conservatives in Congress joined the republicans in opposing these improvements for a better society.

And again, in 1962, his proposal for large scale aid to colleges fell on deaf ears. Also, in 1962 the "Medicare" bill which provided hospital services for the elderly to be paid for by social security taxes took a nose dive.

Another bill, which had so many amendments added to it, also ended up "rock bottom." Its objective was to alleviate loopholes in the federal income tax.

These failures were due, as was noted, to the joint effort of conservative southern Democrats and their colleague Republicans who closed the doors on these measures during his administration.

The northern Democrats did not support Kennedy's bill for public education because he did not include assistance for parochial schools.

Nevertheless, Kennedy did find some success in his foreign policies. Congress did vote funds for his Peace Corps and his Alliance for Progress. In addition, it allowed increase funds for defense and for his space-missile program (he had suggested that the United States put a man on the moon by 1970).

Also he saw his proposal for the Trade Extension Act of 1962 passed. This allowed products of manufacture and agriculture to reach consumers in Western Europe who were becoming wealthy in the exchange of products. By giving the President this authority to negotiate with foreign countries, the transactions with producers helped to reduce American tariffs by as much as "50 percent on some goods and eliminated others altogether."

In August 1963, he signed an agreement with Russia and Britain which brought to a close the testing of nuclear weapons in the atmosphere.

Kennedy was able to pacify the labor unions who demanded wage increases. Secretary of Labor, Arthur J. Goldberg, stepped in to ameliorate the situation of the rebellious steelworkers' demands, and in 1962, they signed a contract that did not contain increase wages. In the same year, several steel companies wanted to raise the price of steel. Kennedy became angered when he got the news and forced the steel companies to rescind their increase prices of steel.

Then, in 1963, he asked Congress to pass legislation which would protect the civil rights of Negroes in employment, voting, and education. Conservative Congressional members took no action thereby holding up the passage of this important bill of the President.

In October 1962, Martin Luther King led a nonviolent demonstration in Birmingham, Alabama. The police broke up this demonstration by using fire hoses and police dogs.

In 1962 John and his brother U.S. Attorney General Robert Kennedy forced the governor of Mississippi and the University there to accept a Negro, James Meredith, as a student. This brought on a riot which was taken down by army troops, United States Marshals, and National Guardsmen.

Another incident occurred at the University of Alabama in 1963 when Governor George Wallace tried to block the entrance of Negro students there. It took the National Guard to force their admission to the University.

It so happened, after Kennedy had made a television address to the nation on civil rights, that Medgar Evers, a Negro civil rights leader, was assassinated.

In 1964, President Lyndon B. Johnson, who was president of the United States, was instrumental in the passage of the Civil Rights Act. "Hallelujah," although it was a long time in coming.

Kennedy's next move dealt with his foreign policy agenda. First, he intervened in Laos when he heard of a Communist takeover. Then, in 1961, when the Vietcong tried to take over South Viet Nam, Kennedy took action by sending 2000 advisers to help South Vietnam establish a democratic, anti-communist government. Later, he increased the force to 18,000. Unfortunately, he died before the war ended. It was under the Nixon administration of 1973, after a loss of 57,000 American soldiers, that our troops were withdrawn from this "hell hole."

The final bell rang when John F. Kennedy was assassinated in Dallas, Texas at the hands of Lee Harvey Oswald, a crazed Russian sympathizer.

It was while he was riding in a motorcade procession through the city in an open limousine with his wife Jacqueline, John Connally Governor of Texas and his wife Nellie, and two Secret Services bodyguards, that a shot was heard from the book depository which struck the President in the neck and cleared his body to wound the Governor. As the President moved forward, another bullet struck him on the right side of his skull. Kennedy's last words spoken were: "My God, I've been hit."

The President's car raced to the Parkland Memorial Hospital where the President was declared dead.

Two days later, as Oswald was being transferred from the police building to the county jail, a strip-club-owner named Jack Ruby pulled out a .38 pistol and shot Oswald in the stomach who later died. Ruby was said to be associated with gangsters. He was tried and found guilty of murder. He was sentenced to death in March of 1964.

There have been many speculations concerning various theories as to how and to who plotted the assassination of President John F. Kennedy. To quell this speculation, the Warren commission, chaired by Earl Warren, Chief Justice of the Supreme Court was established by President Lyndon Baines Johnson.

After five months of testimony and hearings from at least 500 witnesses, the Commission's report stated in September, 1964, that Lee Harvey Oswald had committed the assassination by himself. However, in later years it was revealed that the Warren Commission had failed to uncover all the facts relating to the assassination.

The C.I.A (Central Intelligence Agency) and the F.B.I (Federal Bureau of Investigation) held back information from the Warren Commission. They felt that Fidel Castro and the Mafia were engaged in the conspiracy to kill the President because he and his brother Robert were engaged in a crackdown on these two dangerous subvertists. They felt that their plots to assassinate Castro and the corrupt Mafia would become known. So, a hush-hush policy was devised. Thus, various expansive conspiracies linger on in the minds of people even up to this very day.

The eulogy given by Harold MacMillan, British Prime Minister, expresses the feelings of a nation in sorrow, the United States, when he said: "He seemed, in his own person, to embody all the hopes and aspirations of this new world that is struggling to emerge."

Thus, the life of a great President expired who was dauntless in the throes of danger and determined to do what was right for a country which was trying to emerge from the shackles of poverty, social injustice and heartrending cruelty to a racial minority, the Negro.

MALCOLM X—1965

MALCOLM X WAS A BLACK Muslim militant leader who broke away from the Black Power group in 1963 to form his own organization whose goal was to take charge of their own destines.

To understand where he and his group were coming from, it is necessary to focus on the civil rights movement when Presidents Kennedy and Johnson demanded that Congress form legislation which would enhance civil rights which every American was entitled to. This legislation finally took shape on July 2nd, 1964 when President Lyndon B. Johnson was in office.

The federal government, at this time, took the initiative to advance and protect these rights which were due to the Negro population in the U.S.

Several people led the vanguard to see that these rights were carried out, namely, Earl Warren, the liberal Chief Justice of the Supreme Court, and the Reverend Martin Luther King who addressed a large crowd of 200,000 people who had "Marched on Washington for Jobs and Freedom" in August. A whole host of people of different nationalities and religions, blacks and whites, joined together to give testimony that all men should enjoy the fruits of equal rights and opportunity.

This author would be amiss if he didn't mention Martin Luther King's famous address about his dream: "I have a dream that one day this nation will rise up and live out the true meaning of its creed: 'We hold these truths to be self-evident, that all men are created equal.'"

Other Black Power leaders who also clamored for equal rights, were the radical Stokely Carmichael of the Student Nonviolent Coordinating Committee and Whitney Young head of the Urban League.

Black Power certainly took a twist as defined by Carmichael when he elaborated its purpose as "the coming together of black people to elect representatives and to force those representatives to speak to their needs."

Action was finally made in the political arena in the South for the first time since Reconstruction. This came to light in the 1964 presidential election when Lyndon Johnson received more Negro votes then Goldwater in the states of Virginia, Florida, Texas, and Arkansas. This political force showed up in the South as many minor officers were elected to important positions, such as, state legislatures, commissioners, and local sheriffs.

In 1967, Negroes were elected to a position of mayor in Gary, Indiana and Cleveland, Ohio. This demonstration, evidently, showed that a different attitude was taking place in American society toward the Negro population.

Because of this extraordinary change, the "blacks" began to take an increase interest in black history and black celebrities, such as, Nat Turner who led a slave insurrection in 1831 in Virginia.

However, Black Muslims disagreed with the way things were going and decided to take action. This radical group began to instill among its members a belief in black supremacy and self-discipline. Also, they refused to accept integration in the schools and community.

Some of these radicals even proposed to separate from the white community. They wanted the U.S. government to give them land where they could establish an independent nation.

The life of Malcolm is very interesting and some of his activities should be noted in addition to his involvement in politics and religious matters. He was born in Omaha, Nebraska in 1925 as Malcolm Little. His father was a Baptist minister. In 1946, he ran into trouble with the law and was sentenced to 10 years for burglary. It was during his confinement in jail that he joined the Nation of Islam.

In 1958, he married Betty Shabazz. In 1964, he became disillusioned with the founder of the Nation of Islam, Elijah Muhammad and his philosophy, and also, his corruption; he formed his own organization, Afro-American Unity and the Muslim Mosque Incorporated.

In 1965, he was assassinated by Elijah's cohorts in Harlem's Audubon Ballroom. Three of the assassins were given life sentences. Although there have been various stories as to others involved in the killing, no evidence had been found to link anyone else but members of the Nation of Islam.

Malcolm X's ideas were focused on the rights of black men and the racism that existed among the whites. He told the black people that they should stand up for themselves. However, he suggested violence, if necessary, to achieve their objectives. This attitude irked many whites and emanated a great deal of hostility toward him and the black race. No matter how belligerent he appeared to the public, he still was regarded as a hero among many black people throughout the United States.

MARTIN LUTHER KING—1968

IT CAN BE SAID THAT Martin Luther King got his cue from his exponent, Mahatma Gandhi who ignited the flames of freedom and independence by fostering his ideal of social justice for all.

Luther, an African-American was born in Atlanta, Georgia on January 15th, 1929. He was the son of a minister who became a minister himself. He attended Morehouse College, Crozer Theological Seminary and received his Ph.D. degree from Boston University in 1955.

He, later, became the pastor of the Exeter Avenue Baptist Church located in Montgomery Alabama.

It was at this time that a black woman named Rosa Parks set the fuse that ignited the Civil Rights Movement in the U.S. by refusing to relinquish her seat on a bus to a white man. Immediately, Dr. King took the reins into his own hands and organized a successful citywide bus boycott by black riders.

This incident took national cover and served to launch the Civil Rights Movement.

The segregation of blacks in the South goes back to the old "Jim Crow laws" which referred to any law or practice that separated the blacks from the whites. The term dates back to 1838 when it first blossomed and by the 1880's it became a regular term in ordinary conversation in the U.S. In the 1880's, Jim Crow was a stereotype of a black man who became famous in the Negro song-and-dance performances.

Regardless of the passing of the 14th Amendment to the Constitution back in 1868 which prohibited states from violating equal protection of all citizens, a whole host of segregation laws emanated from the southern states. The intent of these laws was to segregate the blacks from the whites in public places.

Fortunately, these laws were declared unconstitutional in the 1900's by the U.S. Supreme Court. The Supreme Court finally corrected its wrong for, back in the 1800's it actually supported segregation laws at the state level.

This major action by the Supreme Court brings to light the famous case of 1896, Plessy v. Ferguson which the high court (Supreme U.S. Court) upheld the constitutionality of Louisiana's law which required separate but equal facilities for blacks and whites in railroad cars. It is interesting to note that one dissenting vote came from Associate Justice, John Marshall Harlan, who stated, "The Constitution is color blind."

However, this prejudice existed for another fifty years before it was finally stopped.

Two other landmark laws were passed by the Supreme Court in 1954 and 1960 when it rectified two huge cases—Brown v. Board of Education and Boynton v. Virginia.

Both cases denied blacks the equal protection cited in the 14th Amendment.

After having received legal counsel from Thurgood Marshall (later became a Supreme Court Justice, the first black man to hold that post) and support from NAACP (National Association Advancement for Colored People), the Supreme Court issued its findings which stated that the segregated laws did violate the constitutional rights as declared in the 14th Amendment, and therefore, the "separate but equal" doctrine of Plessy v. Ferguson was illegal.

These "Jim Crow" laws did affect the lives of other important blacks, namely, W.E.B. DuBois who became famous as a writer and educator. In 1885, he witnessed in Tennessee actual happenings of these laws which divided the blacks from the whites.

Intimidated by what he saw there, he returned to New England to renew his studies at Harvard University. Later on, he went back to Georgia where he became a professor of history and economics at the Atlantic University.

He is noted for his help in founding the NAACP which led the way in its fight for civil rights.

Another outstanding individual who encountered such prejudice under the Jim Crow laws was a man named John Roosevelt Robinson who made his mark as the first black to sign up with the Major League (Brooklyn Dodgers) in 1947. He, at one time, protested segregation on an army bus for which he was court-martialed. He was, however, acquitted in 1944 and was honorably discharged just before WWII ended.

Last, but not least, a very important American diplomat received a great deal of notoriety when he refused the offer from President Harry S. Truman to become the Assistant Secretary of State. The reason he gave was because he did not wish to subject his family to the harsh Jim Crow laws which had received a great deal of propaganda in Washington, D.C.

Bunche wasn't silent about segregation and spoke frequently against racism. He even went to the extreme in 1944 when he published his book as a co-author, titled: <u>An American Dilemma</u>: The <u>Negro Problem</u> and <u>Modern Democracy</u> which high-lighted the Negro plight in the U.S.

The Civil Rights Movement took off in 1961 after President Kennedy took office.

Then, in 1965, a more militant attitude was focused in the black community. They felt that the movement was taking a dilatory turn. They cited little improvement in housing, employment and living conditions.

The result of this reaction weakened this movement and in its place a Black Power movement emerged pushing for immediate reforms.

At this time, King turned 360° and focused his attention on the poor hoping to unite them and mitigate their suffering and separatist feelings. He, also, included in this campaign the Spanish and American Indians. Then, in 1968, he organized a "Poor People's March" which was to be held in Washington. However, he never lived to see it.

It was at this time that the Watts riot took hold and spread throughout the U.S. These riots caused Luther anxiety and physical pain, as he believed in the technique of nonviolence.

People took vengeance as he was stoned in Chicago, stabbed in N.Y. and was frequently spat upon by dissidents and, even on several occasions, was jailed. He, also, had his home bombed.

Luther was a marvelous orator and his speeches were powerful and effected the emotions and aspirations of his followers.

In the summer of 1963, a massive march of civil rights followers emerged on Washington D.C. It was here that he gave his immortal address . . . . "I have a dream."

His efforts didn't go unnoticed for, on July 2nd, 1964, the Civil Rights Act was passed outlawing all forms of discrimination in public facilities.

Then, in 1965, he was awarded the famous prize, the Nobel Peace award, for his out-standing leadership in the Civil Rights Movement. He was the third Negro and the youngest ever to win it.

The tragedy which shook the nation occurred on the 4th of April 1968, when Martin Luther who had been leaning over a second floor railing at the Lorraine Motel in Memphis, Tennessee while talking to friends below, was shot by James Earl Ray. The bullet entered the right side of his neck. He died an hour later in a hospital.

Robert F. Kennedy's speech of April 4th, 1968 in which he spoke about Martin Luther King, sums up the feelings of people in the U.S. about the shooting of an honorable man: "We can make an effort, as Martin Luther King did, to understand, to reconcile ourselves, and to love, . . . to carry out that dream, to try and end the divisions that exist so deeply within our country and to remove the stain of bloodshed from our land."

At Atlanta's Ebenezer Baptist Church lies King's tombstone on which is inscribed his last famous words: "Free at last, free at last, thank God Almighty, I'm free at last."

ROBERT F. KENNEDY—1968

ROBERT F. KENNEDY'S BACKGROUND HAS been filled with a whole host of tragedies. His elder brother was killed on a bombing mission during WWII, in 1944. His sister Kathleen Cavendish was killed in 1948 in a plane crash in France. His brother John, President of the United States, was assassinated in Dallas, Texas, in 1963. His son, David, died in Florida from an overdose of drugs. His other son, Michael, died at Aspen, Colorado in a ski accident.

Then, on June 5th, 1968, Robert was assassinated at the Ambassador Hotel in Los Angeles, California by a twenty-four year old Palestinian immigrant, named Sirhan Sirhan who gave as reasons for the slaying Robert's support of Israel and his own lavish love of the dispossessed Palestinians.

Robert had just won the California presidential primary after defeating Senator Eugene McCarthy. He was the top candidate of the Democratic Party and was most assuredly to win the Democratic nomination for the presidency.

Robert's assassination has spawned many conspiracy theories which will be related later on in this writing.

Robert was born in Brookline, Massachusetts on November 20th, 1925. He was the son of Joseph and Rose Fitzgerald Kennedy. Joe had made his fortune in real estate and on Wall Street. Later, from 1938 to 1941, he was the American ambassador to England. Rose, on the other hand, had great ambitions for her nine children and saw them attain great heights politically.

Robert, from 1961 to 1964, was the United States Attorney General. He decided to run for the United States Senate so, he resigned this post. He took office as the Senator from New York on January 3rd, 1965.

About this time, near the presidential election of 1968, President Lyndon B. Johnson of the United States was experiencing a period of social unrest due to the war in Vietnam which many United States citizens were thoroughly opposed to. Johnson was trying his best to solve the poverty and discrimination outbursts which were taking place in the major cities of the United States at the time. It was also a period of unrest in these United States cities when Martin Luther King was assassinated in April, 1968.

Robert Kennedy was running for the United States presidency in 1968 and would have beaten Senator Eugene McCarthy who had received a majority vote in New Hampshire against the incumbent President, Lyndon B. Johnson.

After this sad turnout and his declining popularity due to the Viet Nam War, Johnson announced that he had no intention to run for reelection.

Later, Vice President Hubert Humphrey of Minnesota "put his hat in the ring" for the presidency. After the California primary, Kennedy received less votes than Humphrey—393 to 561.

In the presidential race of 1968, the Republican, Richard M. Nixon, won enough votes to secure the role of president of the United States.

Lyndon Johnson's legacy will not be forgotten despite his escalation of the unpopular war in Vietnam. His domestic program, "The Great Society," took hold as he was able to legislate new civil rights laws, funding for those stricken with poverty, and federal aid to education.

Robert gave his state's victory speech in the Democratic presidential primary at the Ambassador Hotel where he was assassinated by a fanatic immigrant, Sirhan Sirhan.

Kennedy's only security was provided by former FBI agent William Barry and two unofficial bodyguards—Rosey Grier, the professional football player, and Rafer Johnson, the decathlon gold medalist.

At the time, the government did not provide protection for presidential candidates only for incumbent presidents.

Kennedy, in order to avoid the crush of his followers, was escorted through the service pantry in the hotel. It was during Kennedy's exit in the kitchen that he was approached by Sirhan who held a campaign poster and behind it a .22 caliber eight-shot Iver Johnson pistol. Sirhan fired three shots, two of which penetrated Kennedy's armpit and the third shot entered Kennedy's head behind his right ear. Kennedy's bodyguards quickly wrestled Sirhan into submission. While they were doing this, Sirhan was able to fire several shots wounding several bystanders.

Kennedy died the next morning at 1:44. As it was mentioned earlier, several conspiracy theories have been reported. It is interesting to note that Rosemary Clooney, the great lyric singer and a strong supporter of Kennedy, was present in the ballroom at the time of the shooting and had suffered a nervous breakdown later on.

Shane O'Sullivan, a filmmaker, allegedly mentioned several CIA officers were present on the night of the assassination.

One such officer by the name of David Morales who was the Chief of Operations was very angry with Robert because he thought that he had betrayed the loyal Cubans who infiltrated the island during the Bay of Pegs invasion to free Cuba of the Castro regime.

Later, O'Sullivan made a documentary called RFK Must Die in which it cast doubts on the earlier identifications of the CIA officers.

The second scenario suggested that a second assailant had been involved in the shooting because of the entry of the shot to the head of Kennedy. However, in 1975, the United States Supreme Court ordered an expert examination of this theory and concluded that there was hardly or no evidence to support this theory.

Another theory involved the Mafia. The killing of President John F. Kennedy was inflicted because the mob sought to silence Robert, the Attorney General, who was incensed with the mob in their crime operations. They assumed the assassination of John would still all the hostile propaganda and campaigning against them by Robert.

The Mafia also thought that the killing of Robert, if or when he became president of the United States, would prevent him from resuming his fight against them.

Sirhan's tie up with the Mafia proved more tenuous than in the case of Lee Harvey Oswald.

Another theory involved the big racketeer, Mickey Cohen. By 1968, Cohen had controlled the gambling rackets in Los Angeles and had controlled the Del Mar and Santa Anita racetracks. Cohen became connected to Sirhan when the latter was the groomer and exercise worker at the Santa Anita racetrack. It was here that Sirhan ran up a huge debt betting on the horses and Cohen found it easy to find someone to do his dirty work who had been engulfed in debt. However, a review of the case involving the Cohen-Sirhan conspiracy theory has become less plausible.

In 1961, Mickey Cohen had been convicted on income tax charges and sentence to prison for 15 years. It was while he was confined in the

Federal Penitentiary at Atlanta that another convict had hit him on the head with a lead pipe which partially paralyzed him. Thus, it has been indicated that Cohen was not in any shape later on in life to get involved with the assassination of Robert. In 1975, he published his biography and died the following year. He was never accused of assassinating Robert F. Kennedy.

The main theory, which does "hold water," is the one in which Sirhan's hatred of Robert was based on Robert's approval for the shipment of more bombers to Israel to fight the Palestinians. This theory has been supported by referring to Sirhan's library card which indicated his take out of many books on the Middle East. Also, it has been reported that his personal discussions with others showed a horrific hatred of the Jews and Israel.

His mission was definitely to prevent the takeover of Palestine by the Israelis and to prevent Robert Kennedy's ascent to the United States presidency.

Robert will long be remembered for his incessant desire to rid the Mafia in the United States and, convict Jimmy Hoffa who was once the president of the International Brotherhood of Teamsters. He too was affiliated with the mob. Also Robert's involvement in the Civil Rights movement showed his concern for the black race.

On June 6th, Robert's body was returned to New York City where he was laid in repose at St. Patrick's Cathedral. His brother, Senator Edward Kennedy, gave the eulogy.

Later on, Robert was transported by train to Washington, D.C. as thousands lined the railroad tracks to offer their respect. Robert was buried in the Arlington National Cemetery near his brother John.

HARVEY MILK—1978

HOMOSEXUALS HAVE BEEN PERSECUTED FROM time immemorial so times haven't changed much. Such was the case with Harvey Milk who was born in New York.

Harvey was elected to the San Francisco Board of Supervisors in 1977. The mayor of San Francisco at this time was George Moscone. Dan White, a former fireman and policemen, who had been elected supervisor under the Moscone administration, resigned his position because he felt his salary was insufficient to support his family, wife and young child.

However, he later changed his mind after being coaxed by some of his friends and confronted Moscone to reinstate him. Moscone, however, appointed a new associate. This action set off a "time bomb". White immediately retaliated and went to Moscone's office where he shot Moscone four times. Not satisfied with this maneuver, he proceeded to Milk's office and killed him—reasons were Milk's opposition to White's return to the supervisor's board and he was a staunch opponent of gay rights.

Milk had developed a fine reputation as a speaker when he campaigned in San Francisco for gay-rights. At this time he had made many friends in the homosexual community and had a firm backing for homosexual rights.

When news was highlighted in the newspapers about the leniency shown White in the jury's verdict of manslaughter rather than of premeditated murder, it set off the spark which ignited the emotions of the homosexuals and they rioted.

White was given a sentence of seven years and eight months in prison—light sentence considering the magnitude of his crime. In 1984, he was paroled. However, in 1985, he committed suicide.

There were several reasons given for White's action. One was his mental condition which was due to his financial problems. The other reason given was because he got "high" on junk food. These reasons were considerably reliable by his defense in the court of law. Evidently, the jury was highly impressed as their verdict indicated. Again, a fine gentleman was gun down before his time due to his sexual preference. Who knows what accomplishments he would have achieved which would have benefited society had he lived a little longer.

JOHN LENNON—1980

It is unfortunate and sad that a beloved individual adored by world fans who was an incredible artist of music, named John Lennon, was gunned down before his time by an insane man, Mark David Chapman. Chapman was born near Fort Worth, Texas, in May 1955, and his family later moved to Decatur, Georgia.

It has been stated that Chapman was a rebellious child. When he reached the age of 16, he became a loyal member of the local YMCA. It was at this time that he found God and changed his behaviors.

In 1977, he took a plane to Honolulu where he intended to kill himself but the attempt had failed.

His stability got worse as he grew older—began praying to the Devil. Later, he married Gloria Abe but, this arrangement didn't improve his stability. She told an interviewer that in a book titled: One Day at a Time, he saw a photo of John Lennon which disturbed his behavior and regarded John as a phony.

Chapman, on several occasions, contemplated killing Lennon but, wavered in his attempts.

However, on December 6th, he had flown to New York and stayed at the Sheraton Center. Then, On December 7th, while there, he hired a prostitute to engage in conversation. This incident was performed because he wanted to imitate the hero of The Catches in the Rye who had done the same thing.

Then, on December 8th, Chapman, who had waited outside the Dakota Hotel that afternoon and evening waiting for John and his wife, Yoko Ono, to return from a recording session, doing Ono's song, Walking on Thin Ice (a new album), approached them as they walked across the sidewalk toward the apartment, and fired five rounds of shots from his gun. Four of the bullets hit Lennon and he fell to the ground, bleeding profusely.

A doorman at the Dakota bounced on Chapman who made no effort to escape. A police car took Lennon to the Roosevelt Hospital but he was already dead.

Chapman pleaded guilty to the killing instead of insanity. His sentence was life imprisonment and solitary confinement.

John's accomplishments and his life must be reviewed in spite of his early demise. John was born in Liverpool, England on October 9th, 1940.

In 1955, he formed a rock band called "The Quarrymen." Later, in 1959, with a joint gesture with his colleague, Paul McCartney, the musical group called The Beatles was formed. Britain was overcome by the publicity and fame of this group of musicians. Also, they were a great hit in the United States.

His love-life took hold when he met the artist, Yoko Ono. However, in order to marry her, he had to divorce his wife, Cynthia. Then, in 1969, the marriage did take place and he "tied the knot." During this time the Beatles broke up. In 1971, he and his wife Yoko moved to the United States. In December, 1980, John at the age of 40 and his wife Yoko began an upsurge in their musical careers. After a lapse of five years, they began to record their music. They settled in New York and occupied an apartment with their son, Sean, at the Dakota Hotel on New York's 72nd Street.

On December 8th, 1980, they encountered a young man named Mark David Chapman who held Lennon's latest album, Double Fantasy. After this meeting, Chapman constantly hung around the hotel seeking a meeting with John.

As stated previously, Chapman shot and killed John outside of the Dakota Hotel.

Fans from all over the world grieved over Lennon's death. He has been honored as a fine musician who had played with the renowned Beatles. Sadly, he had left a dear wife, Yoko and a son, Sean. Nevertheless, he will always be remembered as a fine contributor to the music world.

ANWAR AL-SADAT—1981

PRESIDENT JAMES EARL CARTER'S PRESIDENCY is rated as one of the ten worst in United States history and he is often described as an ineffective and miserable president, who alienated many Washington insiders and members of Congress.[2]

However, Carter did have some significant achievements in foreign policy, such as the Panama Canal treaty, the Camp David Accords, and policies dealing with human rights. Of all these accomplishments, one stands out more vividly and that was the Camp David Accords of 1978. Here, at Maryland, Carter was able to sequester Egypt's President Anwar Sadat and Israel's Prime Minister, Menachem Begin for two weeks. Carter sought to end the war that existed between the two countries.

For the Egyptian recognition of Israel as a separate country, Israel promised to return the occupied land in the Sinai to her which she had conquered in the Six Day War of 1967. In 1982, this agreement was completed. However, the negotiation of the Palestinian refugee problem collapsed.

Sadat was one of thirteen children of a clerical worker born on December 25th, 1918. He took part in a coup that overthrew Egypt's King Farouk in 1952.

In 1969, Nasser appointed him as Vice-President of Egypt. In 1973, he headed the Yom Kippur War with Israel. He wanted to avenge the Arab defeats in the Six Day War of 1967.

As was mentioned earlier, he participated in the Camp David Accords in 1978 when both parties received the Nobel Peace Prize.

---

[2]   Smith, Carter. Presidents All You Need To Know. Irvington, N.Y. Hylas Publishing, 2005, p.24

154

In 1979, Sadat signed a peace treaty with Israel. Nevertheless, skirmishes existed against each other for quite some time until Yasser Arafat and Yitzhak Rabin signed the peace agreement at the White House on September 13th, 1993, in the presence of United States President Bill Clinton.

The signing of the peace treaty in 1979 brought much hatred toward Sadat in the Arab world as they felt the treaty was an act of betrayal. Also, they considered this negotiation a surrender to Zionism. They also considered this act a friendly gesture toward American imperialism. A military parade took place in Cairo, Egypt on October 6th, 1981, celebrating the anniversary of the start of the 1973 Yom Kippur War. Egypt had gained a victory on the east bank of the Suez Canal during this operation.

In the center of the front row of the stands Sadat was given a seat where he could easily observe the entertainment. He was accompanied by Vice-President Hosni Mubarak.

During the celebration, a truck towing a field gun stopped on the parade ground opposite where Sadat was sitting. Out jumped Officer Lieutenant Khaled Ahmed Islambouli who began throwing hand grenades into the stand. A group of soldiers who were located in the truck began to fire at Sadat in the stands. Then, they proceeded to attack Sadat headlong shooting bullets into the crowd. The security guards were unable to react fast enough to quell this onslaught.

Then, as the assailants began their departure, Sadat's bodyguard fired at them, killing one of them. Islambouli and three other of his comrades were captured. The attack had taken its toll. Twenty-eight people were wounded and ten others were killed.

This movement had been traced to the Islamic Jihad, a fundamentalist group who had been repressed by Gamal Abdul Nasser, Sadat's predecessor.

These militants were plotting against Sadat and he was aware of their motive. Therefore, he had, in 1981, 1,500 militants arrested. These arrests prompted an immediate retaliation against Sadat among the militant Jihads. The fundamentalists' objective was to seize power and organize an Islamic state. In order to accomplish this maneuver, they had to create an uprising.

There were several people implicated in the assassination of Sadat. One was the blind Sheikh Omar Abdel Rahman who was later involved in the bomb explosion at the World Trade Center in 1993. Another fundamentalist who took part in this plot was Abdel Salem Faraj, an electrical engineer. He, too, was affiliated with the Islamic Jihad. These assassins were finally brought to trial. Five were sentenced to death and hanged out of twenty-four who participated in the attack. Lieutenant Islambouli and Faraj were included in the hanging.

Sadat will go down in history as a peace maker who signed the Camp David Accords and who was given the Nobel Peace Prize for his efforts in the negotiation.

BENIGNO AQUINO, JR.—1983

BENIGNO SERVILLANO "NINOY" AQUINO, JR. was born on November 27th, 1932 at Concepcion, Tarlac, Philippines. He came from a wealthy family of landlords. His father Benigno Sr. had an important position during WWII in the Japanese government of Jose P. Laurel during the Japanese occupation of the island. His grandfather, Servillano Aquino was a general during the revolution which took place in the Philippines when Emilio Aguinaldo, the leader of the rebels, faced the Americans after they had defeated the Spaniards during the Spanish-American War of 1898. It happened when the United States intended to annex the Philippines that Emilio Aguinaldo, a guerrilla chieftain, decided to attack the Americans. It took three years and required over 60,000 troops to suppress the uprising.

"Ninoy's" mother was Dona Aurora Aquino.

"Ninoy" received a good education. He went to private schools, such as, De La Salle College, Atineo de Manila University and St. Joseph's College. He graduated from San Beda College when he finished high school.

Later, he got a job as a war correspondent working for The Manila Times newspaper and he wrote about the Korean War. He was the youngest war correspondent at that time—only seventeen years of age. He was recognized by President Elpidio Quirino for his journalistic deeds and received a Philippine Legion of Honor award from him.

Because of all this publicity and honorable mention, he became the advisor to the defense secretary, Ramon Magsaysay.

Benigno didn't stop here but, had his sights on better positions.

After studying law at the University of the Philippines (became a member of the Upsilon Sigma Phi here), he decided to seek a career in journalism.

Later, in 1954, his career catapulted in the right direction as he was appointed by President Ramon Magsaysay to serve as his personal emissary to Luis Taruc, leader of the Hukbalahap rebel group.

During heated negotiations, he was able to pacify Taruc and the result was Taruc's unconditional surrender. Again, his career boomeranged as he ascended to great heights at the age of twenty-two when he became the mayor of Concepcion in 1955.

At this time he fell in love and married Corazon "Cory" Cojuangco and they had five children.

Benigno became involved in politics following the footsteps of his grandfather who served under President Aguinaldo and his father who served under Presidents Manuel L. Quezon and Jose P. Laurel.

After he became the vice-governor, he attained the position of governor of Tarlac province in 1961; then, in 1966, he was the secretary-general of the Liberal Party.

He became a political threat to the Marcos government at the age of 34. He became the youngest elected senator in the Philippines.

In February 10th, 1969, Benigno gave a caustic speech in which he denounced Imelda (wife of Marcos) for her extravagance in having a fifty million dollar Cultural Center built which he labeled "a monument to shame". President Marcos retaliated and in a tirade of angry protests and name-calling, he dubbed Benigno "a congenital liar".

However, Benigno's reputation did not flounder as he was selected by the Philippine Free Press magazine as one of the nation's top senators. His achievements labeled him the "Wonder Boy" of politics in the country.

On August 21st, 1971, at the rally of the Liberal Party, two loud explosions occurred at the Plaza Miranda. Eight people died and many others were critically wounded due to the blast. This ignition also set off verbiage between the two which was caustic and also developed a feeling of animosity.

Marcos insinuated that Benigno was involved in the act for the purpose of eliminating his rivals within his party.

However, the police had captured one of the insurgents who was identified as a sergeant of the explosive section of the Philippine Constabulary, a military segment of the government. This man was never heard from again as the military took custody of him from the police department.

On September 21st, 1972, President Marcos issued a decree which enacted martial law on the citizens and immediately had Benigno arrested and imprisoned on false charges of murder and subversion.

Because of a trumped-up trial, Benigno declared that he was going on a hunger strike.

While in a weak condition, the soldiers dragged him to the tribunal meeting. After constant pleas from his family and friends to stop this hunger strike, he finally acquiesced,

Then, on November 25th, 1977, the Military Commission, headed by Major-General Jose Syjuco found Aquino guilty of all charges.

In 1978, despite his internment, he was permitted to take part in the elections of Parliament. At Aquino's suggestion, his supporters organized and ran twenty-one candidates in the Metro Manila election.

It was during this unstable time, that the political party called People's Power, was organized. But, due to election fraud, his candidates lost the election.

In March, 1980, Benigno suffered a severe heart attack, possibly due to his long stay in prison for seven years.

At the Philippine Heart Center, he suffered a second heart attack. The doctors discovered that these attacks were due to a blocked artery. Benigno, fearing that Marcos's acquaintance with the doctors might jeopardize his recovery if surgery were performed, reneged on having an operation performed here and preferred to have it done in the United States. The other alternative was to return to his cell at Fort Bonifacio and die there.

Imelda Marcos made a surprise visit to the hospital where Benigno was recuperating. She asked him if he would like to leave for the United States. However, Benigno had to agree to two conditions—one, to return to the Philippines, and two, he should not speak out against the Marcos government. She then went ahead and arranged his flight and secured passports for him and his family. They were transported to the airport, boarded a plane, and headed for the United States.

At Dallas, Texas, he had the operation and had made a quick recovery.

The Marcos government sent him a message stating that he was granted an extension of stay in the United States.

Benigno, his wife, and children took up residence in Newton, Massachusetts. While in the United States, he received fellowship grants from the Massachusetts Institute of Technology and from Harvard University which financed his work on the manuscripts of two books. To supplement his finances, he also gave lectures in classrooms and auditoriums. In his travels throughout the United States, he took advantage of this opportunity to denounce in his speeches the corrupt Marcos government. On February 15th, 1981, he gave one of his fine speeches at the Wilshire Ebell Theater in Los Angeles, California. Marcos, in the meantime, accused Aquino of being the instigator of a rash of bombings in the Metro Manila area.

Benigno, despite all the threats on his life, decided to return to the Philippines. In order to return to his native land, he and his family had to procure passports. However, his family learned that the Ministry of Foreign Affairs gave orders not to issue them any passports. Also, their visas had expired and renewals were denied.

Nevertheless, Benigno was able to obtain a legitimate passport from a friend who had been working in a consulate in the Philippines.

Again, Marcos interfered and warned all international airlines that Benigno would be denied the right to land in the Philippines. Benigno, being a stubborn man, ignored the threat and boarded a plane at the Logan International Airport in Boston and headed for home.

Benigno sensed a feeling of disaster on his flight back to the Philippines but, he was willing to take the risk for the love of his people and his country.

After he landed, he was escorted by bodyguards, police, and military personnel. Then, the alleged gunman, a man named Rolando Galman approached Benigno and at close range shot him in the head. Galman tried to escape but was immediately apprehended and killed by security guards. The rumor that had spread worldwide was that members of the Marcos government and the Philippine army had plotted his murder.

It was reported that two of Marcos's henchmen, General Fabian Ver the army chief of staff and his colleague, General Luther Custodio the airport security chief, were implicated in the killing.

The result of this diabolical act was a political upheaval in the Philippines and a weakening of the Marcos government. Many of his supporters left his party because of this killing. Marcos's rule took a landslide as he tried to put the blame for the assassination on one gunman.

Marcos called for early elections which he thought would quell the uprisings. Several United States Congressmen who observed the election concluded that Marcos had tried to "steal" the election. The television news had shown the dead bodies of the campaign workers of Benigno's widow, Corazon Aquino.

In the United States, President Ronald Reagan and C.I.A. director William Casey, both of whom had in the past supported the Marcos regime, changed their attitude after viewing all the adverse publicity given to the

Marcos government. Evidently, all this bitter publicity was effective for on February 25th, 1986, Marcos was deposed by an uprising of the people, known as the "People Power" and a segment of the Philippine army.

Marcos fled to Hawaii where he died on September 28th, 1989. Marcos had been ill at the time the assassination occurred, he was recovering from a kidney transplant.

Many theories have been forwarded as to whom was to blame for the assassination. Marcos had been the most likely candidate for the killing as he felt threaten by Benigno's popularity in his bid for the presidency.

Thousands of people gathered in the funeral procession on August 31st. Being a Roman Catholic, a mass was celebrated in his honor by the archbishop of Manila, Jaime Cardinal Sin at the Santo Domingo Church. His body was interred at the Manila Memorial Park.

One good result emerged after the assassination and that was Benigno's wife, "Cory" gained many supporters which eventually gave her the necessary votes for the presidency of the Philippines.

To honor Senator Benigno Aquino, the Manila International Airport was renamed the Ninoy Aquino International Airport. Also, his image was printed on the 500-peso bill. The Philippine Congress enacted legislation in which they declared August 21st as "Ninoy Aquino Day". Several monuments were built in his honor—a bronze memorial in Makati City and another bronze statue in front of the Municipal Building of Concepcion, Tarlac.

The restoration of democracy in the Philippines can be attributed to Benigno's assassination and, most of all, the deposition of a cruel, merciless, despot, Ferdinand Marcos.

INDIRA GANDHI,
PRIME MINISTER OF INDIA—1984

I_T SEEMS UNBELIEVABLE THAT ANYONE_ with the name of Gandhi, who was involved with politics in India, were targeted for assassination.

Indira Gandhi's son, Rajiv was murdered by a bomb blast in 1991 by a disgruntled woman who had carried a plastic bomb beneath her dress.

Mohandas (Mahatma or "Great Souled") was slain on January 30th, 1948 by a Hindu fanatic named Godse who had a gun concealed in his jacket and shot the 78-year-old pacifist in the abdomen. The reason for his vehemence was because Mahatma showed too much tolerance toward the Muslims in India.

Indira was on her way to be interviewed by the British actor, Peter Ustinov who was filming a documentary for Irish television when she was suddenly gunned down by two guards in New Delhi.

Indira Nehru Gandhi was born on November 19th, 1917 to Jawaharlal Nehru and Kamala Nehru and was their only child. Her father, who was tied up in politics, was well known and influential.

Her, mother, unfortunately, was a very sick person who was unable to give a great deal of attention to her daughter while she was growing up. This inattention by her father and mother had a great effect on her personality. She became a loner and had very few friends. Also, to add to this difficulty, her relationship with her father's sisters was practically nil.

When her father was in prison, the police came very often to their home and these callings had a great effect on her personality. At that time, she was only four years old. Her father's quote about these incidents says it all: "I am afraid those early impressions are likely to color her future views about the police force generally."

As she grew older, she became engaged in a movement called Vanara Sena which dealt with young boys and girls involved in the Indian Independence Movement. This organization also helped members of the Indian National Congress to circulate materials which were banned.

Indira, at age 18, witnessed the death of her mother Kamala who died from tuberculosis.

In the 1930's, while attending the College of Somerville and the University of Oxford, England, she joined a radical group whose objective was pro-independence and which was based in London called the India League.

Then, in 1940, her resistance to disease broke down, and she was admitted to a rest home in Switzerland in order to recuperate from a serious lung disease.

While she was in the United Kingdom and touring Europe, she met a young man Feroze Gandhi (an adopted son of Mohandas Gandhi) who was involved in politics. They became close friends and he became acquainted with Indira's mother before her death in 1936.

After Feroze and Indira returned to India, they fell in love and planned marriage. However, the father of Indira did not approve of the marriage because he thought his daughter was too young for such an adventure. He even went to the extent of contacting Mahatma to dissuade their love affair.

However, Indira had a mind of her own and was very adamant and they got married in March, 1942.

Being tied up in politics, they were both arrested in 1942 for taking part in the Quit India Movement. They were both members of the Indian National Congress which campaigned for independence which India gained in 1947.

Feroze became a member of parliament from Uttar Pradesh after India became independent. Indira gave birth to their two sons, Rajiv (who later became Prime Minister of India) and Sanjay Gandhi.

It was at this time that they became separated and shortly thereafter when Feroze was re-elected, he suffered a heart attack. Because of this misfortune, Indira was reconciled to him and they got along very well before he succumbed in September of 1960.

After all this hardship Indira became heavily engrossed in politics. During the 1959 and 1960 elections, she became President of the Indian National Congress.

Then, when her father died in 1964, she decided to work for the Government. She was appointed Minister for Information and

Broadcasting. She was sent to Madras, the capital of Tamil Nadu, to ameliorate the rival factions there and help to reconstruct the area which was in a state of chaos.

Later, she became defiant with the Army of India because they warned her to stay away from the city of Srinagar as the Pakistani insurgents had penetrated near the area. Instead, she aroused the local government and got the attention of the media as to conditions existing there.

After the Pakistani rebels were repulsed, Prime Minister Lal Bahadur Shastri of India, in January, 1966, signed a peace agreement with Ayub Khan of Pakistan. Shortly thereafter, Shastri died from a heart attack.

President Kamaraj's backing and his reputation had the necessary clout to make Indira the new Prime Minister of India. She defeated her opponent, Morarji Desai by a large majority of votes in the Congress Parliamentary Party.

Indira became the first woman Prime Minister of India and the fifth Prime Minister in 1966. Despite Desai's defeat, he did become Deputy Prime Minister of India and Finance Minister.

In 1969, the Indian National Congress split due to the arguments and disagreements with Desai. In 1969, Indira nationalized the banks.

In 1971, Indira got involved in the Pakistani war with India. Because of the enormous atrocities inflicted on the East Pakistani population, millions of refugees migrated to India causing a multitude of problems.

Indira immediately took action because of the instability of the nation of India and the magnitude of problems faced by this influx of refugees from Pakistan. To smooth things out, she took the initiative by securing a Treaty of Friendship and Cooperation with the neighboring country. In 1971, India was victorious in the war with Pakistan and, as a result, a new country was born, Bangladesh.

However, her problems didn't end here. Later on, the two heads of state couldn't reach an agreement over who should rule Kashmir. Eventually, after several negotiations, they finally reached an agreement. She signed the Shimla Agreement with the new Pakistani president, Zulfikar Ali Bhutto. They agreed to solve their differences by peaceful means and through negotiations. The final result of this treaty gave Pakistan a chance to normalize their internal differences and to stabilize the country on a firm footing.

India had been going through rough times agriculturally in the 1960's because of food shortages. Because of government financial support and new innovated agricultural programs, there was an increase in the production of stable products, such as, milk, rice, wheat, and cotton. As a matter of fact, India became a food exporter instead of an importer. This transformation has become known as the "Green Revolution."

Because of these innovations in crop production, which definitely alleviated malnutrition among the populace, especially, among young children, the term "food security" was the slogan given to this program. This advancement in the surplus food supply greatly enhanced Indira's reputation politically in 1975.

In 1967, India became the world's youngest nuclear power. This program stemmed in response to China's nuclear program which India thought was a threat to her safety. Therefore, in 1974, India successfully went ahead and developed a nuclear bomb which she set off near the village of Pakhran in Rajasthan. It went by the code name "Smiling Buddha."

Then in 1971-1975 Indira ran for re-election and a second term as Prime Minister. During her administration in 1971, she faced a whole host of major problems. Her theme for re-election at this time was Garibi Hatao (Stop Poverty). The programs of anti-poverty were intended to give her national support from the urban and rural poor. However, this was not the case, as little money went to alter the poor conditions which still existed in the communities of the poor.

On June 12ᵗʰ, 1975, the High Court of Allahabad declared that her election to the Lok Sabha (lower house of Parliament) was void because of malpractice during the election.

Raj Narain brought charges against her which were accepted by the court and which ordered her to be removed from her position in Parliament; she was banned for six years for running for public office.

However, Indira, adamant as she was, refused to resign and made plans to appeal her case to the Supreme Court. Nevertheless, she was found guilty of malpractice, because she used government machinery for her own use. Also she went beyond the limit of financing her campaign by spending an excessive amount of money.

Despite of all these adverse charges, she still maintained the support of her party and the loyalty of her followers. They stated that her conviction would not affect her career.

In 1975, the Lok Subha took a 360-degree turn when it passed legislation to clear her name of corruption.

Indira appealed the decision of the court and stated that she would continue to serve the people "till her last breath." Huge crowds of protesters demanded her resignation. Indira became an authoritarian when she had the Constitution amended so that the Central Government could increase its power. She, on several occasions, imposed "President's Rule" under Article 356 of the Constitution by stating states ruled by opposition parties as "lawless and chaotic," and therefore she gained control.

In 1977, she called for elections in order to give the electorate the opportunity to show that her administration was for the benefit of the citizens.

Due to charges of Desai (her opponent in the elections) and Jai Prakash Narayan, her popularity diminished and she and her son, Sanjay lost their seats in Parliament. Also their party (Congress) took a firm beating in the elections.

As a result, Desai became Prime Minister and Nielam Reddy became President of the Republic. Indira lost her residence, job, and most important of all, her income.

In June 1979, Desai resigned and Charan Singh was appointed Prime Minister by Reddy.

In later years, Indira was plagued with problems in the Punjab. In June, 1984, Jarnail Singh Bhindranwale's Sikh separatist group had garnered a mass of weapons which they stashed in the Golden Temple (Sikhs holy shrine). The army, ignoring the number of civilians gathered there killed a great number of worshippers. The order she gave was called, <u>Operation Blue Star</u> and was highly criticized by the media throughout the world. Indira justified the attack stating that the objective was to attack the Sikhs who were planning a revolt. Also, she wanted to crush the terrorist, Bhindranwale who had been preaching anti-government propaganda. He was planning to form a separate state called Khalistan.

On October 31st, 1984, in the garden of Indira's residence, two of her bodyguards, Satwant Singh and Beant Singh assassinated her.

As was stated previously, she was to be interviewed by the British actor Peter Ustinov who was filming a documentary for Irish television. Beant Singh shot her three times and Satwant fired 30 rounds. After this incident, Beant was shot and killed and his cohort Satwant was shot and arrested by her bodyguards.

After a four-year trial, Satwant Singh and a third Sikh, a former government clerk, Kehar Singh were executed in January, 1989.

It was also reported that an aid to Gandhi, Rajendra Kumar Dhawan was involved in the plot of assassination. He was dismissed from his post by Mrs. Gandhi's son and successor, Rajiv Gandhi but, due to a lack of evidence, he was later reinstated.

The life of a complex and adamant Prime Minister of India was snuffed out by several vicious Sikhs who desired an independent homeland. The people of India grieved for her loss and remembered her for her loyalty and concern for the welfare of the people and of the country.

WILLIAM FRANCIS BUCKLEY—1985

WILLIAM FRANCIS BUCKLEY WAS BORN in Medford, Massachusetts on May 30th, 1928.

After reading about this heroic gentleman, this author can truthfully say, there aren't enough accolades to express his fortitude and bravery. He received so many medals and medallions from the army, CTA, and civilian personnel for his remarkable feats in the service of his country and afterwards, that only a few will be mentioned here.

For his service as a Colonel in the United States Army, he received the Soldier's Medal, Silver Star, Bronze Star, Meritorious Service, and two Purple Hearts.

Among his civilian awards were the Freedom Foundation Award for Lexington Green Diorama, and the Collegium and Academy of Distinguished Alumni Boston University.

His CIA awards (Central Intelligence Agency) consisted of Exceptional Service Medallion, Intelligence Star, and the Distinguished Intelligence Cross.

In addition to all these distinguished awards, a park was dedicated to his memory—The William F. Buckley Memorial Park in Stoneham, Massachusetts.

C.I.A. Director, William H. Webster eulogized him by saying at his burial service: "Bill's success in collecting information in situations of incredible danger was exceptional, even remarkable".

Buckley's military career was remarkable. He joined the United States Army in 1947 after he graduated from high school. For two years he served as an MP (military police) in the Army. Not satisfied in this position, he decided to attend the Officers Candidate School and graduated as a Second Lieutenant. Then, he extended his military education by going to the

Engineer Officer's School at Fort Belvoir, Virginia. He, also, attended the Intelligence School at Oberammergau, Germany after he had graduated at the Advanced Armor Officer's school at Fort Knox, Kentucky.

Later, he participated in the Korean War and was the company commander of the 1st Cavalry Division.

Later, he enrolled at Boston University and obtained a degree in Political Science.

In 1955, he was employed as an agent with the C.I.A. Then, he became librarian at the libraries of Lexington, Concord, and Winchester.

In 1960, he attended the Special Forces Officers Course, and also, the Basic Airborne outfit. Later, he became the Commander of A and B Detachment groups.

After serving with these commands, he was sent to Vietnam as a Colonel and became the Senior Advisor to the Republican Army of Vietnam.

In 1965, he joined Ted Shackley's C.I.A.'s team which was involved in an assassination program. This employment with the C.I.A. kept him in Vietnam and it was at this time that he became promoted to Lieutenant Colonel in 1969.

After Vietnam, he was assigned to various countries—Egypt, Cambodia, Zaire, and Pakistan.

In 1980, modern writers have stated that he was assigned the task of monitoring the safety of President Anwar Sadat of Egypt who was eventually killed.

In 1983, he succeeded Ken Haas as the Beirut Station Chief at the U.S. Embassy. He was kidnapped by Islamist Hezbollah on March 16th, 1984. Hezbollah was a close ally of Iran.

It was during this trying time that a scandal took place during the Ronald Reagan Presidential Administration. It has been called the Iran-Contra deal which finally culminated in the exchange of missiles for the release of hostages. C.I.A. Director, William Casey, in an attempt to free Buckley, contacted Lieutenant Colonel Oliver North to organize a plan for Buckley's release. North contacted an informant of the Drug Enforcement Administration to buy Buckley's freedom.

Robert C. McFarlane, the National Security Adviser, was told by North that a sum of $200,000 could get the release of Buckley and two American hostages. McFarlane then met President Reagan with the proposal and Reagan agreed.

To obtain this large sum of money, private sources had to be contacted. Therefore, North met the Texas tycoon, H. Ross Perot, a billionaire who provided the necessary cash.

After McFarlane heard about this transaction, he approved the plan and the money ($200,000) was sent.

Then, on October 4th, the terrorist group (Islamic Jihad) revealed the execution of Buckley. To prove that he was assassinated, the Jihad had a photograph published in a Beirut newspaper.

The reason given by the Jihad for Buckley's execution was because the Israelis bombed the Palestinian Liberation Organization base in Tunisia. This, they claimed, was a retaliated response to that incident.

The U.S. National Security Council stated that Buckley probably died of pneumonia on June 3rd, 1985.

Buckley's remains were recovered in 1991 in a plastic sack on roadside near the Beirut airport.

On December 28th, 1991, his body was returned to the U.S. and he was buried in the Arlington National Cemetery. At this time, he was highly honored for his service to his country.

As it was mentioned previously, not enough can be said of this heroic soldier and C.I.A. agent. He served his country well at a time when terrorists were trying to take over other countries which many statesmen have coined as a religious war by a fanatic group—Islamic Hezbollah.

RAJIV GANDHI,
PRIME MINISTER OF INDIA—1991

RAJIV WAS THE ELDER SON of Indira Gandhi and Feroze Gandhi and he became the 7th Prime Minister of India after his mother, Indira died in 1984. She was the first woman Prime Minister of India. He was also the youngest Prime Minister of India when he accepted this position at age 40.

Rajiv was born at Mumbai in August, 1944 when the British ruled the city. His wife was Sonia Maino and they had two children, Priyanka and Rahul. His younger brother was Sanjay Gandhi and it wasn't until after his death in 1980 that he decided to entered politics.

Rajiv came from a famous political family. Jawaharlal Nehru was his grandfather who was instrumental in obtaining India's independence and who became its first Prime Minister in 1947.

Rajiv, unfortunately, was born during a period when his parents were having troubles—both had been in and out of British prisons. Later, the family lived in Allahabad and, also, in Lucknow, where their father, Feroze became the editor of the National Herald newspaper. At this time, the marriage of his parents was unstable so, in 1949, his wife, Indira and their two sons moved to Delhi to live with Rajiv's grandfather, Jawaharlal.

Jawaharlal objected to their marriage because of Rajiv's religion, Zoroastrianism but, they had ignored his objections and eventually 'tied the knot'.

In 1958, Feroze had a heart attack and he and his wife Indira were reconciled during their vacation in Kashmir. Then, in 1960, he had a fatal heart attack and died.

During this period of sadness, Rajiv was attending a private boarding school for boys at the Welham Boys School and later, at the Doon School.

In 1962, he went to Trinity College at Cambridge where he studied engineering. He departed from this university without a degree because of his failure to take the final examinations. In 1966, he left Imperial College, again without a degree.

It was after these engagements that he had met Sonia while she was studying at the Lenox School of Languages and they decided to get married.

Later, he became a professional pilot working for Indian Airlines. This was the time that his mother, Indira, became Prime Minister in 1967.

It was after Sanjay's death in 1980 that his mother, Indira and the Indian National Congress Party coaxed him into politics. At first he refused the opportunity but, later, he accepted the candidacy for Parliament.

In the by-election he won, defeating his opponent, Sharad Yadav. After his election to the Lok Sabha (lower house in Parliament), he became an advisor to his mother, Indira.

She, in turn, was preparing him for the important and famous position of Prime Minister as her successor. To gain fame and popularity of his party, he became the president of the Youth Congress—a step in the right direction.

Then, on October 31ˢᵗ, 1984, a terrible incident occurred. Rajiv's mother, Indira was assassinated by her bodyguards.

Immediately, President Zail Singh urged Rajiv to become India's Prime Minister. Soon after he accepted this position, he requested that President Zail dissolve Parliament and hold new elections. The reason was because the Lok Sabha had finished its five-year term. Rajiv immediately became the official President of the Congress Party.

Because of the Congressional Party's victory, Gandhi obtained absolute authority in the government.

His administrative agenda consisted of improving relations with the United States. Up to this time they had been poor because of Indira's association and friendship with Russia and her leaning toward socialism. Also, her cooperation with members in the scientific and economic fields was shaky. By eliminating bureaucratic restrictions and reducing license fees, he assisted individuals and businesses in the purchase of consumer goods and capital. By exacting these measures, he stimulated the economy of India.

In 1986, he gave a tremendous boost to education by announcing a National Policy to expand and modernize higher education programs throughout India.

In 1986, a central government institution called the Jawahar Navodaya Vidyalaya System sparked the beginning of upgrading the rural education system by providing children from the 6th to 12th grade with free a education. He, also, provided telephones in rural areas where they once were depleted.

In Punjab, Rajiv had internal problems because many civilians thought their civil rights were being jeopardized. Therefore, Rajiv incorporated an extensive police force and army officials to quell the uprising there.

There were critical accusations against the Indian government because it was offering training and arms to the Liberation Tigers of Tamil Eelam rebels who were fighting the government of Sri Lanka. As a result, on July 29th, 1987, a peace agreement called the Indo-Sri Lanka Peace Accord was signed between Rajiv Gandhi and the Sri Lankan President, J.R. Jayewardene in Colombo. The very next day, a bizarre incident happened. Rajiv was struck on the head with the butt of a rifle while he was receiving the honor guard. The man, guilty of this offense, was a Sinhalese naval cadet, Vijayamunige Rohana de Silva. Fortunately, the blow did not kill him. The Sri Lankan President, Junius Richard Jayewardene gave the silly excuse that Rajiv lost his balance and tripped causing the injury. As a result of this uncanny incident, the Indian government failed in its efforts to arbitrate between the Liberation Tigers and Sri Lanka.

About the year 1990, Gandhi's finance minister opened the floodgates of corruption in the Indian government known as the Bofors scandal.

The culprit was Vishwanath Pratap Singh. After his transfer to the ministry of defense, he uncovered payoffs by the Swedish Bofors Arms Company which amounted to millions of dollars which was handled by Ottavio Quattrocchi, an Italian businessman of the Gandhi family in return for Indian contracts. Because of these transactions, Singh lost his position in Congress and his administrative office. Also, Rajiv was found to be implicated in the scandal and exposed by The Hindu newspaper. Then, in 2004, he was given a clean slate and was cleared of this allegation. Singh, his finance minister, because of his allegations against Rajiv became very popular and several parties were organized under his name, one being the Janata Dal Coalition.

Due to these charges, the Congress of Rajiv suffered a major loss. On the other hand, Singh and his coalition formed a government. This coalition, however, didn't damage Rajiv's position as the President of the Indian Congress. However, Singh's government, in October of 1990, tumbled because of Rajiv's influence in promoting Chandra Shekhar, a prominent leader in the Janata Dal party. Chandra, though it has not been proven, became Prime Minister due to Rajiv's Congress support.

For reasons unknown, the Congress withdrew their support for him in 1991.

In January of 1989, Premadasa, the then Prime Minister of Sri Lanka was practically forced to accept the Indo-Sri Lanka Peace Accord. In the 1989 elections, Premadasa was elected President on the basis that the Indian Peace Keeping Force leave Sri Lanka within three months. However, Gandhi refused to withdraw the Indian Peace Keeping Force. He believed that, in order to settle the civil war, Premadasa and the Liberation Tigers of Tamil Eelam, had to be forced militarily to accept the Peace Accord.

In 1989, because of the election of Singh as the new Prime Minister, Indian Peace Keeping Force finally left Sri Lanka only after the peace keeping operation had taken its toll of over 2,400 Indian soldiers.

The last public meeting of Rajiv was at Sriperumbudur on May 21st, 1991 near Madras while he was campaigning for the town's Lok Sabha Congress candidate.

It has been recorded that the assassination was instigated by the Liberation Tigers of Tamil Eelam. A woman, Thenmozhi Rajaratnam, also known as Dhanu and Gayatri, was the suicide bomber who committed the act.

Due to photographs taken at the scene before the murder, police recognized her as the assassin. As she bent down to touch his feet while holding a bouquet of flowers (a Hindu show of respect), she detonated an explosive which killed Rajiv and 16 others from the blast. Her head was decapitated from the blast but it didn't destroy her face.

After an intense investigation, Supreme Court Judge Thomas stated that because of the hatred of the LTTE chief, Prabhakaran toward Rajiv in the latter's involvement in the Sri Lankan civil war, in which he sent an Indo-Peace Keeping force there to quell the uprising and also, because of the insurmountable atrocities carried out by this volatile group against the Sri Lankan Tamils, he confirmed the killing was done unequivocally by Prabhakaran's animosity toward Rajiv. Also, in the Jain Commission report, various agencies and people were named as suspects in the assassination.

At Rajiv's cremation, a memorial statue was constructed in his honor. Also, the International Airport at Hyderabad has been named for him.

A

B

Barrett, Anthony A. <u>Agrippina: Sex, Power, and Politics in the Early Roman Empire.</u>

New Haven, Conn.: Yale University Press, 1996

Black, Jeremy Professor <u>Encyclopedia of World History</u>. London: Dempsy Parr Book, 2000

Blakey, G. Robert and Billings, Richard N. <u>The Plot to Kill the President</u>, New York: Times Books, 1981

Blassingame, Wyatt <u>The Look-It-Up Book of Presidents</u>, New York: Random House, 1996

Bowder, Diana, ed. <u>Who Was Who in the Roman World</u>. New York: Washington Square Press, 1984

Bowman, John, <u>The History of the American Presidency</u>, Edison, New Jersey, Chartwell Books, 1998

Braydon, Henry W., Cole, Charles W., McCutchen, Samuel P. <u>A Free People—The United States in the Twentieth Century</u>, New York: The Macmillan Co., 1970

C

Chambers III, John Whiteclay, Editor in Chief. The Oxford Guide to American Military History. New York: Oxford University Press, 1999

Chubet, Carolyn, Editor. America A to Z. New York/Montreal: Reader's Digest, 1997

Clarke, James W. American Assassins. The Darker Side of Politics. Princeton, N.J.: Princeton University Press, 1982

Commager, Henry Steele, Editor with Cunliffe and Jones, Maldwyn A. The West, An Illustrated History. New York: Exeter Books, 1984

Crutchfield, James A., O'Neal, Bill, and Walker, Dale L. Legends of the Wild West. Lincolnwood, Illinois: Publications International, Ltd., 1995

D

Davison, Michael Worth, Editor. <u>When, Where, Why and How it Happened</u>. London: The Readers Digest Assoc. Limited, 1993

Degregorio, William A. <u>The Complete Book of U.S. Presidents</u>. New York: Wings Books, 1991

Delderfield, Eric R. <u>Kings and Queens of England and Great Britain</u>. Great Britain: David and Charles Publishers, 1986

Diederich, Bernard. <u>Trujillo: The Death of the Goat</u>. Boston: Little, Brown, 1978

Durant, Will. <u>The Story of Civilization, Caesar and Christ</u>. Vol. III, New York: Simon and Schuster, 1944

E

F

Fines, John. <u>Who's Who in the Middle Ages</u>. New York, Barnes and Noble Books, 1970

Fraser, Antonia, editor. <u>The Lives of the Kings and Queens of England</u>. New York: Knopf, 1975

Fuhrmann, Joseph T. <u>Rasputin: A Life</u>. New York, 1990

G

Garrod and Lofthouse Limited. <u>Britain's Kings and Queens</u>. London: Pitkin Pictorials Ltd., 1974

Gerard and Del Re, Patricia. <u>History's Last Stand</u>. New York: Avon Books, 1933

Gibbon, Edward. <u>The Decline and Fall of the Roman Empire</u>. New York: Penguin, 1977

Grant, R.G. <u>Assassinations</u>. Pleasantville, New York: Toucan Books Ltd., Reader's Digest Book, 2004

H

Hammerton, Sir John and Barnes, Harry Elmer, editors. The Illustrated World History. Vol. 2, New York, 1940

Hart, Michael H. The One Hundred, A Ranking of the Most Influential Persons in History. New York: Carol Publishing Group Edition, 1995

Horan, James D., Sann, Paul. Pictorial History of the Wild West. New York: Crown, 1954

Huie, William Bradford. He Slew the Dreamer. New York: Delacorte Press, 1970

I

J

K

Knauer, Kelly, Editor. <u>Great Events of the 20th Century</u>. New York: Time Book, 1997.

Knauer, Kelly, Editor. <u>Time 100 Leaders and Revolutionaries, Artists and Entertainers</u>. New York: Time Inc. Home Entertainment, 1998

Knowles, Thomas W. and Lansdale, Joe R. <u>The West that Was</u>. Avenel, New Jersey: Wings Book, 1994

L

Lanning, Michael Lee. The Military 100. New York: Barnes and Noble, 1996

Law, Jonathan, Editor. 1000 Great Lives. New York: Carroll and Graf, Inc., 1996

Liberati, Anna Maria and Bourbon, Fabio. Ancient Rome, History of a Civilization That Ruled theWorld. New York: Barnes and Noble with White Star S.P.A.2004

M

Mallet, Michael. <u>The Borgias</u>. New York: Barnes and Noble, 1969

Marks, Anthony and Tingay, Graham. <u>The Romans</u>. London: Usborne Publishing Ltd., 1990

Massie, Robert K. <u>Nicholas and Alexandra</u>. New York: Atheneum, 1967

McKinley, James. <u>Assassination in America</u>. New York: Harper and Row, 1977

McMillan, George. <u>The Making of an Assassin</u>. Boston: Little, Brown, 1976

N

Newark, Tim. <u>Where They Fell</u>. New York: Barron's Educational Series, Inc., 2000

O

P

Q

R

Radzinsky, Edward. <u>Alexander II: The Last Great Tsar</u>. Freepress, 2005

Riasanovksy, Nicholas V. <u>A History of Russia</u>. New York: Oxford University Press, 1984

Roberts, J.M. <u>A Concise History of the World</u>. New York: Oxford University Press, 1995

Rodgers, Nigel. <u>Ancient Rome</u>. London, England Hermes House, Anness Publishing Ltd

S

Schweikart, Larry and Allen, Michael. <u>A Patriot's History of the United States</u>. New York: Penguin Group, 2004

Sifakis, Carl. The Mafia Encyclopedia. New York: Facts On File, 1987

Smith, Carter. <u>Presidents, All You Need to Know</u>. Irvington, New York: Hylas Publisher, 2005

Smith, Jean Reeder and Smith, Lacey Baldwin. <u>Essentials of World History</u>. New York: Barron's Educational Series, Inc., 1966

Sykes, Sir Percy. <u>History of Persia</u>. London: Macmillan, 1930

T

Tuchman, Barbara W. <u>The Guns of August</u>. New York: Macmillan, 1962

U

Ulam, Adam B. <u>The Bolsheviks</u>. New York: Collier Books, 1976

V

Vaughan, Donald. <u>The Everything Civil War Book</u>. Avon, Massachusetts: Adams Media, 2000

W

Wenborn, Neil. The U.S.A. a Chronicle in Pictures. New York: Reed International Books Limited, 1991

Williamson, David. The Kings and Queens of England. New York: Konecky and Konecky, 1998

Wilson, Colin. A Criminal History of Mankind. New York: G.P. Putnam's, 1984

Woodward, Bob. Veil: The Secret Wars of the CIA 1981-1987. New York: Pocket Books, 1987

X

Y

Young, George F. <u>The Medici</u>. New York: Modern Library, 1930

Z